The Climate Emergency Plan

A Revolution in Activism

by

RON KOSS

ii

The Climate Emergency Plan: A Revolution in Activism

ISBN: 979-8-218-76373-2

A Prayer for Charles Franklin Koss

May your life benefit from our collective action today.

May you discover and express your own potential to benefit those who will follow you.

Contents

Author's Note

What notable experience and background prompted me to articulate this vision for *The Climate Emergency Plan?*

Why, with so many prominent and oft-quoted scientists, academics, policy experts, and celebrity activists generating so much content today, would or should you make room to consider my not-so-prominent nor oft-quoted voice?

Sometimes breakthrough ideas and innovation come from unexpected places. Often, the tried and true does not deliver the bold and needed.

Case in point, organic baby food, a $11 billion product category today, was not born from the tried-and-true big companies at the time, like Gerber, Beechnut, and Heinz. Rather, it came about via an outsider who imagined in 1976, at age 25, a world with fewer pesticides supported by an organic foods industry that didn't exist at the time.

I was that outsider doing the imagining. The company I founded in 1987 with my twin brother Arnie was Earth's Best, the first organic baby food company in the United States. The "Organic Foods Industry" I envisioned almost 50 years ago, now has a presence in almost every supermarket in the United States.

I believe the climate activist community needs to shift gears to have a greater impact. A "revolution in activism" necessitates the leveraging of our capitalist economic system to make more money for the common and greater good. Most will agree that minimizing the impact of global warming is for the common and greater good. This leveraging, however, may seem an improbable leap, but the case is made in the following pages that it is not impossible.

What follows in *The Climate Emergency Plan* are my ideas and concrete plans to do this work and make that needed shift.

Please note that throughout the following text I have frequently used two forward slashes // to stand for the word *PARALLEL*. The intention was both to not over-use the word "parallel," which becomes important in this writing and to suggest the idea of creatively building the forward slashes representation into a future trademark.

Dedication

To the millions across the globe who are resilient in their hope and determination to meet the global warming crisis.

To the many who will answer the call and come together to form a movement, a mighty bucket brigade of small and large actions that add up to a transformation of how we live and consume on our Earth.

To the "impossible" which may be a door to unimagined horizons and not just a ceiling that declares the limitations of our human potential.

AND

To the millions who will be displaced, the many who will die, suffer, and live lives without the stability and security of the Earth's planetary life support systems.

To the species that will become extinct because of climate change.

And to all the future prayers, tears, and trauma needlessly spoken, shed, and felt …. IF we humans choose to react to tragedy rather than act to prevent it.

Preface

The *Climate Emergency Plan* that follows below may be described by some as "Magical Thinking." This diminishment is both exasperating and to be expected. Exasperating because our present lives are surrounded by the magic of – once upon a time - Magical Thinking.

Cross the North American continent by jet in 5 hours – Magical Thinking to everyone living in the 18th century.

Hold something in your hand like a phone and talk to someone else 10,000 miles away – Impossible!! More Magical Thinking.

Peace on Earth – Is that Magical Thinking?

What is possible and what is not? What is real and what is not in the realm of our senses and understanding?

Humankind does not have a uniform and conforming realm of senses, perceptions, and conceptions.

We can imagine what is possible. We can judge what is possible. But we don't know.

Countless times, the impossible has been proven to be possible. Countless times, so-called Magical Thinking was not delusional or fantastical, but rather a glimpse into the future.

So, what are our limits and what limits us?

How certain are you in your judgments?

And regardless, if the possible is failing us, what is the impossible that would not?

A "Revolution" connotes disruption, upheaval and often violence. Not the case in this context. Here, a "Revolution" is intended to be more like the change of seasons in Vermont from winter to spring – gradual with dramatic swings of warmish to freezing cold, but determined and inevitable day by day.

The transition from a fossil-fuel powered world and a global economy that sacrifices its carbon storing treasures like the forests, jungles, mangroves, and marshes to keep growing itself does not offer the naturalness and unquestioning acceptance of a season change.

Hence, there is no inevitability to it. But there are some overlaps.

First, a response to our warming globe is needed as is the necessity for the end of winter, rebirth, and the beginning of the growing season to sustain life as we know it.

Second, the transition to responsible stewardship of our planetary life support systems will not bring instant results like the flip of a light switch. Like the change of seasons, it will also be gradual and day by day. There will be the ebb and flow of progress. But the season of reducing atmospheric carbon and stabilizing global temperatures will eventually arrive.

Third, spring seems an impossibility when everything lies still, grey, cold, and lifeless. And so will the ideas of this Revolution in Activism amidst the bleakness of our post-2024 election. But spring always prevails. With your engagement, so will this *Climate Emergency Plan.*

"When a

complex system

is far from equilibrium,

small islands of coherence

in a sea of chaos have

the capacity to shift

the entire system to a

higher order."

Ilya Prigogine

Nobel Prize- winning chemist

Introduction

<u>There are no vaccines for climate change.</u>

What happens when the 7,000,000 acres of Central Valley ag land in California can no longer be supported by the irrigation system that makes it all happen? What happens when we start running out of water because we've pumped out the aquifers and climate change reduces the capacity of the 60,000 square mile Central Valley watershed?

What happens?

Nothing good given that half of the fruits, vegetables and nuts grown in the United States are from that Valley.

Covid gave us a taste of an unthinkable scale and scope of disruption. People died alone as family members grieved from afar. Public funerals and memorial services all but disappeared. Hugs, kisses, and handshakes were unsafe. Schools unsafe. Restaurants unsafe. Travel unsafe. Living as we knew it, unsafe.

It happened, but the light at the end of the Covid tunnel finally showed up.

However, when the oceans rise because the Greenland ice sheet is melting unprecedently and irreversibly, there will be no light at the end of the low-lying Miami Beach and New Orleans's tunnels. Low lying Bangladesh may lose approximately 11% of its land affecting 15 million people by 2050.

Desertification caused by climate change and land mismanagement, such as overgrazing and unsustainable freshwater use, threatens the food security now of more than 2 billion people.

Rising CO_2 and methane levels and increasing ocean temperatures are causing ocean acidification. Many marine ecosystems hang in the balance.

The global warming tunnel relative to our relatively short human life spans is forever dark.

There is a disaster reel waiting in the wings for our children and grandchildren and so on.

Is climate catastrophe still too much of an abstraction? If Covid was not a wake-up call to not only the possibility of catastrophe but the experience of it, what would be?

If the possible is failing us, what is the impossible that would not?

Forty-nine years ago, in 1976, I read Rachel Carson's 1962 book *Silent Spring* that documents the environmental damage caused by the indiscriminate spraying of the pesticide DDT. It made me feel sick, sad, and dis-empowered. What could I do?

A big impossible idea magically jumped into my (at the time) 25-year-old being – organic baby food. I imagined baby food as the best way to grow the hodge-podge of small organic growers scattered across the country into a movement to counter pesticide spraying.

Eleven years later, in 1987, in Middlebury, Vermont, my twin brother Arnie and I launched the first organic baby food company in the U.S. – Earth's Best. This big idea has made and continues to make a difference, along with the many other organic foods companies that have followed over the years into the marketplace.

The *Climate Emergency Plan* that follows below is another impossible idea that jumped out at me after reading a disturbing April 3, 2019 open letter to the British daily newspaper *The Guardian*. A dire statement within that letter and its signatories surprised and alarmed me.

"The world faces two existential crises, developing with terrifying speed: climate breakdown and ecological breakdown. Neither is being addressed with the urgency needed to prevent our life-support systems from spiraling into collapse."

Bill McKibben, Greta Thunberg, Naomi Klein and 20 other climate activist leaders

Again, what could I do? Feeling disempowered, one penetrating question arose from the ashes of my despair.

If the possible is failing us (and it is), *what is the impossible that would not?*

<u>Why read another book on the climate crisis?</u>

In 2021, Microsoft founder Bill Gates wrote a well-reviewed *"How to Avoid a Climate Disaster- The Solutions We Have and the Breakthroughs We Need."* It has a primary focus on technologies as the key to solutions. Is technology the impossible that will not fail us?

Hannah Ritchie published in 2024 *"Not the End of the World – How We Can Be the First Generation to Build a Sustainable Planet."* Hers is a data driven and positive approach that asserts that carbon emissions per capita are down; that deforestation peaked back in the 1980s; and that our air is vastly cleaner than it was a generation ago. In other words, we are making progress and the "possible" is really not failing us.

Naomi Klein, on the other hand, in her 2015 *"This Changes Everything – Capitalism vs The Climate,"* challenges us to abandon the core "free market" ideology of our time, restructure the global economy, and remake our political systems. Is this the impossible that will not fail us?

There are many others. Stories of activism, innovation, adaptation, displacement, and intervention; treatises that push back against apocalyptic environmentalism and even deny climate change itself.

Why this book? Because, as Bill Gates acknowledges, technology is necessary, but not sufficient to address our global warming crisis.

Because data, as Hannah Ritchie wields and invaluable as it is, only reports on quantifiable results reflecting our actions, but does not interpret it or offer us an ethos that guides and directs us.

Because we are globally entrenched within the capitalist economic system and its free market ideology. What this means for the climate is that since the Paris Climate Agreement, from 2016 – 2023, the world's 60 largest private banks financed fossil fuels expansion to the tune of $6.9 trillion US Dollars with the six largest US banks – JP Morgan Chase, Citi, Wells Fargo, Morgan Stanley, and Goldman Sachs – accounting for over $1.8 trillion.

It is far more likely that the core "free market ideology," as it currently operates, will kill us before we decide to abandon it.

If so, we need a transformational expression of that capitalist free market ideology, not all of it, a piece of it. And we need a collective urgency expressed as never before – A Revolution in Activism. What could that look like?

The Climate Emergency Plan.

PART 1

We are the Impossible that Will Not Fail Us

Chapter 1: Nose down. Landing gear up.

Although I am capable of magical thinking or at least capable of being accused of it, I do not have a Magic Wand to wave to bring this *Climate Emergency Plan* to life.

I am not sure if anyone mortal has one of those, but a magic wand – small "m" small "w" – yes, those are in the hands of a relative few.

MacKenzie Scott, who gifted in 2021, $2.7 billion to 286 high impact organizations; another $2 billion in 2024; and $19 billion since 2019 – has such a magic wand. She alone, with her personal resources and her connections, could alter the title of this little book from *"The Climate Emergency Plan"* to *"A Climate Emergency Plan Start-up"* – Applications being Accepted.

What follows are big ideas in search of a village of magic wands. A money wand or wands and the hearts that generously gift money are, of course, needed. But money, to be of value, needs something of value to propel.

I hope you will find something worthy of being propelled – a plan to unify climate activism into an empowered de-carbonizing and re-wilding high-profile happening – a Climate Activist Movement (CAM) – fueled by – a *PARALLEL //* Economy – singularly dedicated to making such an all-encompassing activist movement financially possible.

The uniting of this scale of mobilized and united global CAM activism with a committed and focused economic engine – a *PARALLEL* Economy – is the *Climate Emergency Plan* we need to build together to stop our faltering.

The Plan's aim is to unify climate action organizations into a "League" of sorts like Major League Baseball (MLB) and the National Basketball Association (NBA). Imagine individual climate focused "teams" working in a more coordinated, prominent, and effective whole – as a League, the *Global Climate League.*

If that metaphor does not work, consider that of a Union – an entity that brings people together who have a shared interest in a specified outcome. A labor union brings people together to improve benefits, salaries, and working conditions. Imagine the *United Climate Union.*

But this *Climate Emergency Plan* is more. It can also be a powerful economic engine in its own right - a connector, a facilitator, and a catalyst. The Plan aspires to be an organizing entity, a neural network that brings not-for-profits, activists, philanthropists, scientists, celebrities, influencers and the general population at large together to more effectively de-carbonize and re-wild and defend our planetary life support systems.

One of the benefits of this coming together will be financial empowerment and independence. The *PARALLEL* Economy will strengthen the financial foundation of climate change activism. World Wildlife Fund, The Nature Conservancy, Green Peace, Rainforest Alliance, Environmental Defense Fund, Sierra Club and many others will deliver more supercharged impact. That impact will not be just because of the support of *PARALLEL* Economy generated money. It will be the money plus a mobilized army of coordinated activism that births, starting with you and me, this empowered movement.

Climate Action, all of it, is falling short.

This *Climate Emergency Plan* is not the typical entrepreneurial idea seeking investors. It is not another not-for-profit idea competing for money and members. And it is not important that the *Climate Emergency Plan* be the name or that the *PARALLEL* economy with its //™ logo be designated as such, although it could be. It is a response to a recognition of grave import.

Earth is warming. This warming is accelerating. Life, as we know it, hangs in the balance. And these understandings are now common knowledge to many, if not most.

There is one more important understanding.

Climate action, all of it, is falling short. We face a unique dilemma – an airplane that we Earthlings are all riding on has its nose pointing steeply down and its landing gear is up. This is not a good configuration for an airplane. And we know it! Media reports filter down to us regularly. CO_2 concentrations are at record levels. The Amazon Rainforest is under attack.

One-hundred-year floods happen every year. Some gloomy version of "Nose down, Landing gear up" is always the headline. And we carry on as we are carrying on, without the urgency or agency to sensibly right the plane that no one should want to be on, but that no one can get off.

Why don't we level the plane's nose so we're not catastrophically heading toward the ground and put the landing gear down so we can escape this peril and land the damn plane, bumpy as it will be?

Is it because we don't know how? Or is it because we are resigned to its impossibility and our real task is to forget about fixing the plane, face the music, and prepare for the worst?

Chapter 2: Is the world just a business?

I remember listening to a 2020 podcast that General Electric produced called *Cutting Carbon*. GE is one of the premier manufacturers of turbines that electrify the world.

As I listened, I was struck by an explanation that conventional thinking accepts as a matter of fact. One of the GE speakers explained that there are established technologies available to sequester carbon at a scale that might be consequential to combat rising CO_2 levels. But he went on to say that the "commercial drivers" are not in place to propel the use of these technologies to the prominence that is needed.

Is the world just a business? Some say that this is an immutable law. The "powers that be" that are dictating our climate change story are obviously dedicated to making money. It does not appear to matter to them whether the plane we are all on crashes. There will still be money to be made after the crash, maybe even more than ever. The term "Disaster Capitalism" has already been coined.

Who are the "powers that be?" Are they the amalgamated nature and impact of the stock market? Big oil money and the like? Are they the push and pull of behemoth wealth like that of the Koch brothers and tech-giant Elon Musk? Are they the dominating influence and pervasive effect of super-powers like the United States and China? Are the "powers that be" also immutable?

Even if the "world is a business" is a fixed point of reality, and I don't know that it is, the "powers that be" are not immutable. They are formidable, but their strength, that is their clarity of purpose to make money, is also where the door to many possibilities lies. Money is money, whether it is made by sequestering carbon or burning fossil fuels.

What if the perception of opportunity shifted? What if leveling the plane's nose (de-carbonizing) and bringing the landing gear down (re-wilding) presented itself as the most compelling near, mid, and long-term money-making opportunities?

Impossible? At first glance, it is a big idea to swallow. But a second look shows favorable and encouraging reasons for the perception of business opportunity to shift. Climate change is undeniably upon us. It can't be reduced to fears stoked by political and activist elites because the record heat, record fires, and record drought are affecting hundreds of millions of us around the globe. Los Angeles is burning apocalyptically at the time of this writing.

"Favorable and encouraging" are the reasons for my hope and the birth of this proposed *Emergency Plan*. It is not a utopian conception. Capitalism does not disappear. Rather, it is "we" who appear in force to catalyze into existence those commercial drivers that will, in turn, quicken the transformations necessary to meet the global warming challenge.

The Climate Emergency Plan focuses on how-to manifest this collective "we" and how to empower it..... and to do so now.

It is a big idea in need of a band of unified and empowered organizers and creative problem solvers. And that is who I hope some of you, the readers, will become. The leaders of this Revolution; the warriors; the healers; the bridge builders and the visionaries.

Also essential is the "most of us," the "we" that are unique and magical in our own right but are not holding the kind of wands found in the hands of people of great wealth like MacKenzie Scott and Bill Gates or influencers, like Oprah and Michelle Obama. I hope you, the most of us, will also somehow discover this little book and be ready to come together to become the next wave of "powers that be."

Miraculously, every part and piece of the *Climate Emergency Plan* already exists, just not put together as a working whole. We don't have to wait for technologies to mature like commercial fusion power or imaginations like time travel to actually materialize. There are no mountains to climb like that. It is doable and now.

What this Revolution in Activism and all of its potential is waiting for, believe it or not, is just us.

And here lies the epic plot twist in our human story. The producers in this planetary drama we've all been dropped into have cast us as more complex and mysterious than fusion power and time travel will ever be.

You see, "we" are the impossible that will not fail "us."

Chapter 3: What's missing?

Bill McKibben, one of the Guardian Newspaper signatories, wrote in his 2019 book *FALTER*:

We're the only creature who can decide not to do something we're capable of doing. That's our superpower... So, yes, we can wreck the Earth as we've known it...as we're doing right now. But we can also not do that. We could instead put a solar panel on the top of every.... roof.....and if we do, then we will have started in a different direction.

I do not know that we will make those choices. I rather suspect we won't – we are faltering now, and the human game has indeed begun to play itself out. That's what the relentless rise in temperature tells us.... But we could make those choices. We have the tools (nonviolence chief among them) to allow us to stand up to the powerful and the reckless, and we have the fundamental idea of human solidarity that we could take as our guide.

Back then I wondered, what would drive us to the ethos that "we're all in it together," to that "human solidarity," that Bill refers to? What would organize the world in such a way that there was sufficient urgency to overcome cynicism, die-hard individualism, and undermining resignation?

How do we advance the ubiquity of solar panels and build a super-charged non-violent movement to re-wild and de-carbonize on behalf of everything we hold dear?

Is it fantastical to think that there are answers to the above questions obedient to the time constraints we seem to be faced with?

This is where I knew I wanted to begin – with the answers.

I embarked on a journey exploring what might lead us from faltering to enduring; that would lead us away from individual silos of action and towards a unified climate and ecological movement, one of the two beating hearts of the *Climate Emergency Plan* introduced here.

<u>Become the powerful</u>

The sobering plea for "urgency" made by luminaries like Bill, Greta, and Naomi, most connected to climate activism, spoke the obvious to me – something essential is missing in our response to the climate crisis. The extraordinary efforts of yesterday and today are proving insufficient. We are faltering.

What is missing?

It is this. The ecological crisis is declared, but the action response, in total, is not a "crisis action" response. It is diffuse. It is piecemeal. It is not unified. The parts do not add up to a discernible whole.

Yes, there are plenty of organizations to join but there is no singular movement. There is no bucket brigade in motion galvanized in solidarity and connected to a unified intelligence kicking-butt. Rather, there are thousands of independent initiatives constantly looking for money and throwing as much of it as possible onto problem "fires" that become territories of action. This approach is not working sufficiently. There is another way.

Indivisibility and unity of action is a known inspirational collective human response to crisis if all or many are thrown into it together. There is plenty of climate action and advocacy today, but there is no Climate Activist Movement (CAM). It is needed. It is possible.

What if coupled to this CAM inspiration is a *PARALLEL* Economy, the second beating heart of the *Climate Emergency Plan*. Together, working hand in glove, their shared and singular purpose is to birth and buoy a climate emergency response – that metaphorical bucket brigade into action that re-wilds and de-carbonizes with the urgency needed to write an alternative ending to our human-made climate crisis story.

Bill McKibben writes in *FALTER* that "we have the tools to stand up to the powerful and reckless." The *Climate Emergency Plan* sets out with the same objective and an additional one – to also become the powerful.

We need a short cut.

Too many people today are sitting on the sidelines thinking, "What can I do?" or "This isn't my problem." "I'm too busy." "I don't matter" or "What problem?" or "It's already too late."

Many are resigned to believing that big corporations' control everything; that the political process will never solve the problems; and what's my membership in Green Peace or NRDC or WWF or 350.org really going to do?" To others, the climate crisis remains an abstraction or is invisible. "I can still buy tuna fish. Gas is up, but not crazy up. There are seashells on the beach. The geese are migrating. Yesterday, it was -15F" … and so on.

We need a short-cut to activate and direct this vast amount of untapped collective potential sitting on the sidelines that is either resigned, indifferent, or unaware. We need to find our way to that urgency to delay, if not stop our faltering. And if that way is not to just "stay the course," with activism strategies as they are and our economic paradigm as it is today, what is it then?

It may be this *Climate Emergency Plan*.

It may be that we have to re-consider what we think is impossible.

PART 2

The *PARALLEL //* Economy

Chapter 4: The *PARALLEL* Economy is not a business Idea.

The *PARALLEL* Economy, in its simplest expression, is a climate activist driven economic model that runs parallel to our current broken profit addicted capitalist system. It solely exists to re-direct consumer and commercial purchasing power towards de-carbonizing and rewilding to slow down if not reverse the global warming trend.

PARALLEL is not a dictate or an "ism" nor does it require the dissolution of traditional capitalism. After all, why make things difficult? The *PARALLEL* Economy conception aims to compete with that "ism" and prevail by winning hearts and minds in the broadest sense – by building the biggest tent possible. The foundational ethos of the *PARALLEL* Economy is inclusion, that is, building alliances anywhere and everywhere. This is the only way to succeed.

The future we need will not manifest around a polarity such as we are the good guys and the profit seeking folks are the bad guys. Rather the future we need will manifest around reducing that polarity and expanding the understanding of what success is and then how to achieve it. Ideally over time, the parallel realities will get closer and closer together until they appear to have merged. That will be success.

The inclusive spirit of a *PARALLEL* Economy is also infused with toughness and determination

This is not a contradiction. The // journey will not be a walk in the park. The "Welcome Mat" is not going to be out until the battle for hearts and minds is won or at least until the tide has perceptibly turned. Emphasis in this paragraph is on the word "battle" as in "will," the will to find a way to build a movement to stop our collective faltering.

The *PARALLEL* Economy will obviously still depend on capital but rather than secure it from traditional profit seeking investors, *PARALLEL* will uniquely and creatively rely on philanthropy and borrowing.

To re-emphasize, the *PARALLEL* Economy per se is not a "business" idea. It is a practical solutions-oriented initiative. Although it will encompass many businesses, its raison d'etre is not to be a business. This is because money making in the ordinary sense is driving us all into a ditch. So, what's the point of doing that if we know where we are headed?

Getting Started

Imagine a *PARALLEL* choice for banking and credit cards. Why not make our collective money work full-time for climate change activism. Why not re-direct trillions of dollars of our purchasing power and capital for the planet and become part of the global warming solution?

But how?

We create, over time, a free market *PARALLEL* Economy with a singular focus – All *Profits to support Global Warming Activism.* We unite our monies in our everyday living as a global movement. We co-operate. We identify friendly philanthropic dollars and add our own purchasing power and capital. We do the impossible. Not all of us. Enough of us.

Entrepreneurial ideas such as this need to be well matched to the readiness of the market waiting for those ideas. Without this readiness, no matter how great the idea is, progress will be stalled. With this readiness, the seemingly impossible becomes possible.

The global yearning for solutions to the climate crisis is vast. The readiness for a more mobilized collective emergency response is obvious. A *PARALLEL* free market economy united by a single focus – global warming – is possible. Why not start now?

The *Climate Emergency* Bank *(CE-Bank)*

We start with the *Climate Emergency* Bank, probably a digital bank at the outset. It might be a cooperative, B-Corp, or perpetual trust legal entity. A founding leadership board of directors – a wheel with many spokes of expertise – is formed.

And a simple road map to build this bank is crafted. Simple means principled, focused, incremental, and innovative.

The founding principles are crystal clear.

The *Climate Emergency Bank* has one focus: Meeting the global warming crisis.

There is only one stakeholder: Planet Earth (its life support systems and all life)

It has a charter with two goals: All net profits will be directed to de-carbonizing and ecological restoration actions.

And there is one measure of success – Delivering impact.

There are plenty of precedents for starting banks, even innovative, socially responsible, and activist driven ones.

Consider the B Corp Amalgamated Bank – stating on its website – *"we don't just have a mission; we're on a mission to be America's socially responsible bank."* Second, the Florida based *Climate First Bank,* founded in 2021, offers a vision *"to reimagine finance as a force for good and become the most impactful bank contributing to the drawdown of atmospheric CO_2.* A third example is the Fortbright Bank headquartered in Chevy Chase, Maryland with a declared mission *"to curb climate change and help build a sustainable future."*

Perhaps there are collaborative opportunities with these existing banks and starting a bank is unnecessary. That remains to be seen. The main point here is that a dedicated bank with a focused mission to finance climate change activism is essential.

The 30,000' View

The *CE-Bank* will underwrite a credit card – The *Climate Emergency Card* and offer a lending program – *Climate Emergency Lending (CE-Lending)* dedicated to the purpose and vision of its one stakeholder – Planet Earth. The *CE-Bank* will also have a charitable giving arm – *Climate Emergency Giving (CE-Giving)* that provides grants to decarbonizing and restoration initiatives.

Becoming Big

Imagine the *Climate Emergency Bank* growing into an international alliance – the *Climate Emergency World Bank Alliance*. Its credit cards, lending programs and charitable giving have become global in scale. New foci appear like educational initiatives. A social media platform develops and becomes unrivaled.

Money is power and energy. Too much power is in the hands of those who are near-sighted and exploitive. Not enough energy is available to support climate change activism and planet-purposed entrepreneurship in the profound ways needed. This is a problem. The *Climate Emergency Bank* is offered as part of the solution. It would provide a conduit for both aligned philanthropy and consumer and commercial capital to support de-carbonizing and ecological restoration actions.

Philanthropy

Philanthropy is integral to addressing one of the undermining factors that limit access to capital for necessary climate technologies, innovations, and IMPACT programs. That factor is the inherent aversion to risk by traditional banking.

One unfortunate result of this aversion is the so called "Valley of Death" – the desolate place that promising enterprises, who are perceived to be too risky, get stranded. Another nail in the coffin of enterprising initiatives shows up with skeptical investment professionals pricing debt at interest rates that prove to be deal-killers. A third related result is that early-stage technologies, even up and coming industries, cannot handle investments at the enormous scale needed to attract major investor players.

By force of habit the banking system is restricting the financial agency needed to meet the demands of the climate crisis. As a result, too much promising potential is falling through the cracks. This loss is contributing to our faltering. It is unacceptable.

To address this limiting factor (risk aversion) that thwarts research and development, testing, scale-ups and market penetration, the *CE-Bank* would aim to leverage philanthropic dollars to make bank lending viable to targeted business enterprises, environmental programs, projects, conservation land acquisitions and the like.

Risk cannot be ignored, but it is also a tired excuse for the status quo to persist and vital opportunities to be ignored or to languish. This is a perfect place for focused philanthropy to play a pivotal role as a catalyst to shift the perception of risk, enable more enlightened lending (and ultimately investment) and have much more impact than it ordinarily does in its traditional role.

The Climate Emergency Credit Card

The aim is to build a global climate change movement. Although it is counter-intuitive to suggest the "buying of things" as the uniter/igniter to do this, here is why it can be.

Everyone in the developed world is buying things using credit cards. You don't have to become a member of an organization to do so. You don't have to march or strike or declare yourself in any particular way. Trillions of dollars are being exchanged. Servicing and championing that exchange is a profitable banking economy. That economy, virtually the "be-all and end-all" of life on developed Earth, is the obvious genesis of our climate crisis but the not-so-obvious doorway (or at least one of the doorways) to its solution.

The *Climate Emergency Credit Card* (backed by the *CE-Bank* and eventually the *CE-World Bank Alliance*) has the potential to be an instantaneous conduit to activism, a global community, and a movement. Holders will use it virtually every day. They will have an impact every day. They will belong to a community around the world sharing the same intention. There could be tens of millions of cardholders. More. Why not?

Together, cardholders will manifest, through what is ordinarily just the invisible business of banking transactions, more of the "brute cash" or the muscle needed to do the work of ecological restoration and de-carbonizing that is not getting done because there is never enough of it. With the *Climate Emergency Credit Card*, this dynamic changes.

The aim is for the card to become a champion and a focal point for a global "Take Back the Climate Movement." In doing so, it will be a unifier and offer to many a much-needed sense of awakened kinship. It will uniquely empower millions to join hands to insist that the "buying of things" play an important role in the "fixing of things."

Simultaneously, the effort will be dedicated to transforming consumerism such that it is more aligned with the health of our planetary life support systems, the future Earth, and its future generations.

The power to generate the brute cash and have the muscle to move the entire globe is within "our" power. We don't have to wait on anyone or anything! This united movement wants to happen.

Here are some of the early indicators.

In 2019, the Swedish financial company *Doconomy* launched the "Do Card" which tracks carbon emissions related to a cardholder's purchases and offers consumers options to buy carbon offsets. Switzerland's *Cornercard* similarly includes a climate calculator. Japan now has a credit card capable of visualizing CO2 emissions based on payment data.

There is also an established way for not-for-profits to offer their own credit cards. It is through a commercial banking enterprise known as "Charity Affinity Credit Cards." For example, there is the *Green America Rewards VISA* card (greenamerica.org); the *International Living Futures Institute VISA* (living-future.org); and the *Salmon Nations Reward VISA* (mycommunitycc.com). Typically, these Affinity Credit cards offer about one-half of a percent to the non-profit for every purchase.

Encouraging also is the aforementioned Florida based full-service *Climate First Bank* with assets now (February 2024) surpassing $540 million and solar financing of $87.4 million (43,000kW). Through its *1% for the Planet* commitment, *Climate First Bank* gave $124K in 2023 to environmental not-for-profits.

On the one hand, it is heartening to know that juxtaposing the climate (and other socially responsible initiatives) with a credit card is more than just another pie-in-the sky big idea.

On the other, how do we make it more impactful and engaging than: *I took a trip and paid for it with my Cornercard. In turn, I bought, or they bought for me carbon offsets somewhere in the world. I feel less guilty.*

How do we improve upon a financial model that only returns $5000 to a participating non-profit on a million dollars of credit card sales? Or in the case of the *Climate First Bank* that aligns itself with the *"1% for the Planet"* model and in 2023 returned $124,000 to environmental not-for-profits on a calculated $12,400,000 ($124,000/.01) of profit.

To be clear, what's in place is important because directionally it's a step. It represents a growing consciousness. But arguably what is in place is not generous enough. It is not urgent enough. It is not ubiquitous enough.

What if, for example, the *Climate First Bank*, the *Amalgamated Bank,* the largest B Corp bank in the U.S., and the *Forbright Bank,* one of just seven U.S. banks that is a signatory to the United Nations Principles for Responsible Banking, each with its environmental stewardship missions, united to build a high profile and impactful climate revolution banking "movement?"

Sadly, I believe this is unlikely. Mission driven banking, as important and admirable as it is, suffers from the same blind spot that mission driven environmental organizations are afflicted with – that is the recognition that their business-as-usual model, no matter how earnest, progressive and diligent it might be, is not and will not catalyze the urgency needed to stop our collective faltering.

To divert attention away from this recognition of collective faltering is to either be resigned to it, or to avoid acknowledging it, or just to see it differently.

What I am certain of is that Olympic caliber brainstorming on the subject is needed. I am certain that this is not the moment for business-as-usual. And what I know is that the heart of the solutions to the problems we face lie in our numbers, our votes, our courage, our faith, our unity, and our collective brute cash.

All tied together is how we will make a difference. Impossible? I don't think so.

Climate Emergency Lending CE-Lending

Climate Emergency Lending is the foundation for a more enlightened expression of capitalism. Why not transform as much of our economy as possible with a dynamic *PARALLEL* lending arm? That is, lending solely dedicated to supporting ecological restoration and de-carbonizing actions.

Why not take aim at challenging the axiom of perpetual growth by offering an alternative to it?

We do this by deploying a significant niche of capital available to *CE*-Lending and make it work for the planet/us. We do this by financing new choices for millions around the globe who are anxiously waiting for a new, more enlightened ways to plug their lives into sanity. We give those who want to stand apart from the lemming stampede they find themselves entrapped in more ways to do so.

The only way to do this is to create the financial wherewithal to support an economic paradigm that will do the transformative work of values-driven entrepreneurship. And this needs to be done with a Marshall Plan-like dedicated focus.

It is not the strongest of the species that survives, nor the most intelligent; it is the most adaptable to change. Charles Darwin

Will we adapt in the face of faltering and lacking the urgency needed to protect our planetary life support systems?

Climate Emergency Lending is one good hopeful reason to answer, "Yes."

Climate Emergency Giving

The need is obvious, and the premise is simple – direct a portion of the *PARALLEL* Economy's "profits" to support global activism campaigns in every major affected eco-system. There are myriad possibilities, so priorities would be identified, and meticulous focus applied for maximum impact utilizing the granularity produced by the work of the *Climate Activist Movement (CAM)* and its global climate action plan outlined below in Part 3.

CE-Giving might result in the acquisition of large tracts of critical habitat around the globe and the underwriting of initiatives/programs that help to reduce local economic pressures in critical bio-regions that lead to deforestation, over-fishing, species extinction and other ecological stress points.

CE-Giving might focus on catalyzing solar applications throughout the developing world. This would be a complementary grant program to *CE-Lending* initiatives.

As the *Climate Emergency World Bank Alliance* establishes itself, the reach and IMPACT of its Global Giving campaign would also expand.

PARALLEL Kool-Aid?

I am not channeling a Pollyanna-like distorted optimism. I am not envisioning a "changed" world in any absolute sense. Our present, non-*PARALLEL* economic reality will not magically disappear. Everyone is not going to drink the // Kool-Aid. There will still be an "us" and "them." There will still be climate change deniers, bad-actor corporations, waste, and economic injustice. But there will be markedly less of that, and the balance of power will start to tip in the // direction.

Why? Because the newly connected dots will present themselves as a tangible and dynamic choice that does not feel diffuse and ephemeral. They will present themselves as that BIG tent with many portals of entry. The opportunity to be a part of something empowering, and hopeful will be plain to see.

There will be a great attraction to both the ease of participating and the accompanying gravitas of a *PARALLEL* Economy as a game-changer when it is perceived. The global yearning for solutions to the climate crisis is becoming vast. The readiness for *PARALLEL* is growing every day. A *//* free market economy united by a singular focus – global warming – is possible.

Momentum will grow exponentially when the first *PARALLEL* Economy toeholds appear, like the *Climate Emergency Credit Card*. Moments of action will become integrated more and more into the *PARALLEL* economic movement.

A *//* reality choice will become our norm and the era we are in now will recede into the past and become known to those in the future as the *Age of the Near Miss* – the time when we mistook freedom for license. The time when we mistakenly thought that "or" was the conjunction between living free and dying as in "Live Free or Die" rather than "and" as in "Live free and Die." The time when we fiddled while our planet burned. The time when the bucket brigade – the Climate Activist Movement and *PARALLEL* Economy – showed up at the last minute. Nearly a disaster – A Near Miss.

In our *PARALLEL* life, the united global climate activist consumers' movement will certainly serve if not dictate corporate priorities and actions. The Law of the Jungle says so. Capitalist behaviors will either serve the wishes of those who feed it, or it will perish.

PART 3

The Climate Activist Movement

Chapter 5: It only takes a moment.

There are two sides to the *Climate Emergency Plan* coin, the *PARALLEL* Economy introduced above in Part 2 and the Climate Activist Movement (CAM) introduced here.

This is how a Revolution in Activism happens.

The Climate Activist Movement (CAM) is an idea, an imagination that I believe is needed and is possible with a lot of creative and skilled collaborative input.

The revolution starts with formalizing a conceptual agreement between scientists and activists. Let's call it the CAM Agreement (CAMA). In fact, it is already formed in spirit via many international environmental collaborations and loosely expressed within academia via consensus reports published by the Intergovernmental Panel on Climate Change (IPCC, a UN body established in 1988).

CAMA not only represents an envisioned foundation for a global plan of climate action, it also delivers the nuts and bolts – a road map for re-wilding and de-carbonizing.

But the CAM Agreement is not the Paris Climate Agreement.

Paris has not succeeded in creating the urgency needed to preempt the writing of the dire 2019 open letter published in *The Guardian*. Certainly, it represents ground-breaking progress, but it has not coalesced as a unifying force of action capable of being independent of controlling influencers like national identity, power politics and big-business interests.

The Paris Climate Agreement captures a wish, an aspiration and even offers a road map, but has not proven to have the teeth and hence impact needed to be the gamer-changer we collectively need.

The wisdom of what we already know and the intention to abide by that wisdom is too often obscured and sidelined by forces and dynamics that persist in wielding ultimate power. These forces are much like dinosaurs doomed to extinction but still wreaking their havoc to the bitter end.

We need a momentous shift in who or what holds ultimate power. In my view, it must be wielded by a mobilized global populace with its angst and pent-up potential energy finally united and released in a movement of Climate Revolution activism coupled with Consumer Revolution economic activism. Efforts like the Paris Climate Agreement should serve as prologue for the next waves of transformative action.

Remember, if the possible is failing us, what is the impossible that would not? Answering this question is imperative. Most, if not all, ideas/impulses in response to the imposing challenge facing us will naturally seem far-fetched and unwieldy – impossible, in a word. However, in this *Climate Emergency Plan* conception "impossible" is not the end of the road, but rather a hopeful beginning.

Habituated thinking and the resistance that accompanies it is exactly what inertia depends on to keep things the same, no matter that the same, regarding our global climate, is akin to a determined lemming march to the cliffs edge and over.

The Heart

At the heart of the Climate Activist Movement Agreement (CAMA) is a dynamic international team that will lay out an elaborate schematic of interconnected ecological flash points, ongoing actions, and key organizations and scientists involved – from global to local. The CAM team identifies and prioritizes an agreement for actions so that the "potential" human energy on our planet (i.e. you and me) knows how to organize and where to go to be that virtual revolutionary bucket brigade. Re-wilding and de-carbonizing at scale are imperative.

To be clear, the aim is not to re-invent the wheel. Starting from scratch is not an option. An inclusive series of symposiums across the globe uniting activists, philanthropists, celebrities, environmental groups and scientists needs to be initiated or re-initiated. Collaborations, for example, with such climate mitigation efforts as *Project Drawdown* (founded in 2014 by Paul Hawken and Amanda Ravenhill) and the work of the Buckminster Fuller Institute are integral to formalizing CAMA. Coordination with 350.org,

Natural Resources Defense Council, The Nature Conservancy, Environmental Defense Fund, Green Peace, the Sierra Club and others are a given.

This activist movement plan, when it is ready, needs to be brought to the public in spectacular fashion – the biggest of debuts. The event needs to be a compelling, inspiring, and unifying call-to-arms; a BIG BANG moment of creative expression, clarity of purpose, possibility, know-how and of course public relations that must overcome inertia, cynicism, and dis-empowerment to galvanize the world with its ambition and focus. This has never happened!

The debut will showcase a compelling agreement – that both supports and builds upon the productive actions and initiatives that are already in motion and will provide a re-focused, re-prioritized and re-vitalized blueprint for the world community to meet the climate and ecological crisis with the needed urgency.

Most importantly, the Climate Activist Movement (CAM) represents a united declaration of action. It will create the over-arching purpose for the next generation and the next: A Globe in Crisis – meets – A Globe in Action. Organizational silos do not disappear, but they are now in service to a greater whole and a unified effort.

To be clear, it is not that governmental actions, laws, policies, and enforcement worldwide will become irrelevant in this conception. That would truly be Pollyanna-ish. They, of course, will remain essential. But within the *Climate Emergency Plan* lies another force, an organized and unified one with economic and political clout and the potential to be influential, if not a game-changer in our global warming story. That other force is us.

What stands in our way? – the SO-SO force.

SO-SO

Every idea seeking to answer the question, "What is the impossible that will not fail us?" goes up against a force like gravity. Let's call it the "SO-SO-Force." "SO-SO" for Same Old-Same Old. It is invisible. It is ever present and seemingly invincible. It is the force behind declarations like "there isn't the money" for what is needed. It is the force that pushes us toward silos, sides, sameness, and separation. It is the force that breeds cynicism and defeatism. But unlike the force of gravity, which is immutable here on the planet surface, this SO-SO-Force is not. And few seem to know this or many have forgotten it. It can be resisted and even overcome by a superpower we each have: the power of our "free-will" as human beings.

Free-will gives us the choice and capacity to transcend the constraints of our human nature, as well as our personal, social and cultural histories, and our ingrained habits. Lemmings do not have this super-power, which makes their collective stampede to the cliff's edge and over still puzzling, but not preventable. We humans do have this power which gives us the choice to veer away from the climate cliff that faces us now.

Coupled with another super-power, our "skillful-will," we have the capacity to not only make these transcendent choices, but also to skillfully connect them (using our intelligence, creativity and adaptability) to actions that can realize just about any aspiration.

The Climate Activist Movement Agreement (CAMA) intends to be an expression of these super-powers, our human potential. It represents the brains and delivers the global activism road map to meet the climate crisis. With this Agreement in hand, a consumer/people's movement driven by empowered hopefulness and inspired action is possible. The PARALLEL Economy side of the coin represents the know-how and means to become the economic brawn or power needed to drive this road.

Remember, standing up to the powerful and reckless is necessary but not sufficient to meet the climate crisis. Becoming the powerful, by creating a movement that is also an economic juggernaut, must happen.

More on the Road Map - The CAM Agreement (CAMA)

To fill this in a little more, re-wilding initiatives might be broken into 8 primary areas of activism (Forestlands, Grasslands, Mangroves, Salt Marshes, Peatlands, Deserts, Oceans, Seabeds). Each primary area would be mapped out in elaborate depth. This map is "live." It is accessible to everyone. It is user friendly so anyone that is interested can broaden their understanding and participation. It is updated in real-time by thoughtfully configured designated oversight teams.

For example, mapping "Mangroves" means the identification of each key mangrove area across the globe; the status of each area; the organizations involved in each area; the projects in motion and/or planned; the key scientists and activists engaged; an assessment of the local communities affected; identifying the local leaders involved; results to date, problems, concerns, and recommended actions; and related critical paths.

For mangrove area by mangrove area, this work is meticulously done by an international team built by the CAM leaders and supported financially by mobilized philanthropy and the budding *PARALLEL* Economy. The proposed mapping builds upon existing work and will be expanded upon and updated. Again, there is no reinventing the wheel intended. There are projects in Central Java and Suriname that are having success. There is the *Mangrove Action Project* that uses the *Community Based Ecological Mangrove Restoration Approach* that emphasizes local community participation.

There is much that has been learned and much learning to apply.

With the updated mapping complete, a "Summary for Mangroves" will be written, and a priority list created that directs, as part of this activist revolution, the "potential energy" in the form of humankind waiting to be a part of a "from-the-bottom-up" unified movement of action. Some of this potential will be expressed as money; some as local direct-action in affected areas; some as extensive outreach via media; some as research and monitoring; some as lobbying; and so on.

A projection of the expected outcomes is detailed for any given action as is the related timeframe and how it will be measured and monitored. A chain of command is identified including oversight. Also, built-in redundancies are added to problem-solve to help ensure functionality, and to improve the probability of delivering results.

The same body of mapped information will be created for each primary area. When assembled, the CAM Agreement (CAMA) will represent the web of life mapped across the globe and framed as crisis areas needing re-wilding. In turn, the related priorities within each primary area will be specified and plans of action mobilized to meet those priorities down to the last detail.

The degree of coordination and alignment (and money) required to accomplish all the above may seem daunting and unachievable. Perhaps, but I believe it is possible because there is an alchemy to all of this waiting for its moment.

<ins>It only takes a moment.</ins>

Case in point, from my perspective as a U.S. citizen, the December 7, 1941 Pearl Harbor attack galvanized sacrifices by all to defend freedom and defeat tyranny. Life in America back then was filtered through one lens – the common good for the war effort. There were scrap metal drives by children and victory gardens; rationing of gasoline, heating oil, shoes, clothing, coffee; and the sacrifices of millions of U.S. service people, of which 416,800 gave their lives. A collective brain manifested in the twinkling of an eye and an alchemy to direct the energy flow followed. It was war.

Is the climate crisis as big a threat to our way of life, to our very lives, and what we hold most dear as that infamous December day that united us 80-plus years ago?

For some the answer is "yes" and for others "no" or "I don't know." And there lies the rub. Climate change, unlike Pearl Harbor, is not a single comprehensible event with a clear enemy to mobilize against. "CO2 is invisible and an abstraction. Global warming is a disconnect when it is -20F outside. The coral die-off on the Great Barrier Reef means what to our everyday lives?

More than 2400 people died at Pearl Harbor. There was no ambiguity about who the enemy was or what the response should be. It was a simple 1+1=2 calculation.

For those who answer "yes" to the perceived threat of climate change, the gravity of the ongoing "attack" on the natural world and our planetary life support systems is also a 1+1=2 calculation. It's a Pearl Harbor situation x 100 or a 1,000,000 with a big "but." BUT without a unified crisis response to rally around and for.

This writing appeals for the necessity of a crisis response and makes the case for how to manifest it – that is how to make the threat to humanity understood by many more as a devastating attack with everything that's cherished on the line. It is a call to all to help create the collective brain and brawn needed to manage and direct the vast amounts of information and potential energy inherent in such an all-encompassing mobilization.

We need this unifying moment of organization and commitment simply because, although battles are being admirably won in the fight to meet the climate crisis, the war is being lost.

Moments or a Movement?

Presently, there is plenty of response to climate and ecological degradation. There are ground-swell activist movements like *Extinction Rebellion* and *YouthStrike4Climate*. There are dot.orgs galore and NGOs (non-governmental organizations) and Summits and Conferences and United Nation's Committees and miscellaneous Compacts, Accords, Agreements and dire warnings.

And millions of citizen contributors.

We are surrounded by each other, running by and beside each other, constrained by discrete silos and limited by discrete actions. We are up against far more powerful forces like corporate greed and nation by nation "feel-good" pledges, political gamesmanship and calculated self-interest. And time is running out.

My aim here is not to ignore the important unifying efforts that are in motion today. *Earth Day* is a global phenomenon celebrated by more than a billion people every year. *Youth Strike 4 Climate* is inspirational and compelling. The *Global Climate Strike* is a needed call to disrupt business as usual. There is a lot striving in motion orchestrated by amazing and dedicated people.

But what we have mostly are unified moments – flashes of brilliant light. What we need is a unified movement – brilliant light 365 days a year. This is the "impossible that will not fail us."

Why Impossible?

Because obviously, some would say, a unified movement is a naïve notion. The world is too complex. There are too many organizations; too much politics; too many countries; too much big money; too many egos; too much inequality; not enough bridges to transition to a new economic paradigm; and too much disruption and sacrifice required.

My response to the above starts and stops with…… if a unified movement is the impossible that will not fail us then let's get on with it.

Chapter 6: Getting on with It.

Political scientist and professor of public policy at the Harvard Kennedy School, Erica Chenoweth, writes in her 2011 book, *Why Civil Resistance Works* that for non-violent mass movements to succeed, a minimum of 3.5% of the population needs to unite in a vocal and sustained way. Although her research focuses on outcomes related to political change and the overthrow of oppressive regimes (i.e., Civil Rights Movement; Marcos in the Philippines), it does point to the "possibility" of revolution latent in non-violent resistance/action.

Dr. Chenoweth notes that people are social animals; that change is exciting and contagious; and that the status quo can shift in perception very quickly if a sustained and compelling groundswell of resistance, advocacy and action reaches a tipping point.

I believe we can reach this tipping point by re-organizing already existing "waves" of activism such that they come to meet the shore (the masses) in more coordinated sets with their amplitude (impact) maximized rather than random one-off events and splashes of attention with relatively little, long-lasting effect.

We need these big waves. Waves of the future: kids – students; Gen Xers, Millennials, Gen Zers; Waves of celebrity; Waves of musicians; Waves of scientists and activists; Waves of engaged corporations; Waves of wealthy individuals; Waves of united environmental organizations; Waves of consumer activism; Waves of leadership nations; Waves of big first initiatives; Waves of entrepreneurial responses; and Waves of targeted non-violent civil resistance.

And each set needs to be followed by another and another – many big, all coordinated, all a part of a united movement responding to a shared perceived crisis guided by some semblance of a collective brain. The visibility of each wave set will stimulate interest, combat cynicism, evoke hope, and encourage people to find their place of engagement within the climate revolution.

All orchestrated and coordinated by whom?

I know there are seemingly endless "But hows?" or "What about this and what about that?" Those questions are natural and of course necessary, but not yet. Discovering the impossible that will not fail us requires the discipline to be patient and to suspend disbelief until you no longer have to.

This united movement wants to happen. Conditions are exquisitely ripe. Every day, it seems there is another cataclysmic declaration – species extinction – Amazon rivers are drying up – rapid decline of the natural world. The good news, however, is not so obvious. The potential energy, mostly invisible to us, is also expanding exponentially in response.

The planning needed to organize and coordinate the many waves of human expression mentioned above to create such a unified movement may be invisible to us today, but as Dr. Chenoweth says, *"change is exciting and contagious and if a sustained and compelling groundswell of resistance, advocacy and action reaches a tipping point, the status quo can shift very quickly."*

All orchestrated and coordinated by whom then? By the creative and organizational intelligence that the Climate Activist Movement conception will inspire; leadership, in a word.

This leadership capability and know-how certainly exists. But why would I ever think people are going to use that know-how to unite as a movement sufficient to dramatically impact corporations and government policy making and spending on scale, for real? That has not happened today or ever, why would it suddenly happen tomorrow?

Why wouldn't I think like this?

There are tens if not hundreds of millions of people world-wide concerned about climate change right now and billions more potentially waiting in the wings. There is an aligned scientific community. There is a vibrant and growing activist community. There are international youth organizations that are flourishing. Corporations are always looking for the next frontier and will follow like a puppy if there is food/opportunity in front of it. And there is tremendous philanthropic wealth in place accompanied by its potential to catalyze the changes that it is inspired by.

Moment-makers, organizations like 350.org, Green Peace and NRDC, have been doing the hard work of climate crisis education and battling on behalf of the environment for decades. They have been ceaselessly striving to transform their efforts into the necessary impact that would be sufficient to protect our planetary life support systems.

Despite the dire April 3, 2019 open letter in the British daily newspaper, The Guardian, that alarmed me so, the efforts and actions of these moment-makers have manifested many of the "ingredients" necessary for the *PARALLEL* Economy and CAM movement being fleshed out in these pages to emerge. You don't have a movement without these moments.

The only thing standing in the way is believing that it is possible.

I see it.

I am certain that many have yearned for some version of the unified inspiration I am trying to convey here. Bits and pieces of the *Climate Emergency Plan* have been emerging for years. Youth for the Climate; Strikes for the Climate; and the Climate Action Network International, a global network of more than 1900 civil society organizations in over 130 countries stand out.

At the 2023 United Nations Climate Change Conference in Dubai (COP 28 – Conference to the Parties), there were 85,000 participants, including 150 Heads of State and Government, Indigenous Peoples, youth, philanthropists, and international organizations in attendance. Although not legally binding, there was agreement on:

- New funding for climate related losses and damage
- Enhanced global efforts to strengthen resilience
- Linking climate action and nature conservation
- Ramping up practical climate solutions.

The Climate Emergency Plan | Ron Koss

The recognition that the fossil fuel era must end was also declared at COP 28, and not by a bunch of Green New Deal zealots, but by the global community at-large. The impulse to unify as a human species to address global warming is fact. That impulse is surrounding us and yet somehow it remains in the background of our everyday lives

It's like watching something trying to materialize in the Star-Trek transporter room. It's there, but it's not yet there. Can you make out what is betwixt and between?

I can. I see it. It is something like this *Climate Emergency Plan*. It is wave after wave of children with their parents' support engaged to fight for the best future they can have; followed by waves of young adults fighting for their futures; and Baby Boomers fighting for their children, grandchildren, and their legacy.

It is a big transporter room. Also, betwixt and between, is the future Earth.

That miraculous "ball" is in our court – every one of us.

If we focus where the climate movement is weak and fix it; if we brainstorm a new paradigm to make it more unified, inclusive, and powerful; if we also keep creating moments of brilliant light, then we will fulfill our potential as human beings and we will know what is possible.

I believe it is more than we think.

Chapter 7: Dropping deeper into the weeds

The Weeds

Moving from the abstraction to some imagined details or "weeds" is important.

Imagine there are 200 critical ecological crisis or flash points, call it the "A" list. And there are 500 on a less critical "B" list and 1000 more on a "C" list. Each "hot spot" has a story that is told and the environmental impact of each is documented with some brought to life, David Attenborough style. It is all made relatable and compelling.

Examples of "A" list foci might be replacing hydroflurocarbon (HFC's) refrigerants that have the capacity to heat the atmosphere 1000X more than CO_2. Reducing food waste is another critical flash point. Tropical forest restoration, family planning, renewable energy expansion and addressing the complexities of managing cattle and other ruminants all require immediate and dedicated attention.

An Individual Environmental Action Plan (IEAP) is then crafted for each crisis point with target reduction goals of *CO2* identified; net implementation costs estimated; and operational savings over-time projected. Paul Hawken's *Project Drawdown* is already doing this with its *"100 solutions to reduce global warming."* We are well on our way.

Also, equally critical metrics would be generated to show the estimated costs to build "bridges of security" for populations adapting to changed environmental priorities and new economies. Resources would be quantified in each IEAP report to meet the needs of the poorest, the least responsible for damages, and the most affected by climate change.

Imagine that all this action is captured by a team of global "storytellers" who are social media wizards. Successes are reported as are failures. The climate fight is made transparent. It becomes easy to follow crisis points of interest. Maybe there is *"Climate TV."* It is easy to see how to be involved. It's easy to feel part of a united movement. It is exciting to feel momentum and be hopeful.

What I am envisioning is a vast web of circulating energy, that is the many millions of us worldwide who care about climate change, coupled with a responsive nervous system or leadership community spanning the globe on behalf of the climate, the planet, and all of us who care. Call it communication, education, and activism working as one vital body, one *Climate Emergency Plan* being.

What is clear is that national boundaries have faded into irrelevance. Pollution that is happening in China, the United States, Russia, India, and Japan does not abide by random lines drawn on a map. The entire globe is warming, not just the countries that are polluting it the most.

The 305,823 square miles (and counting) of Amazon rainforest sacrificed over the past 40 years to cattle raising, soybean production and logging (an area about twice the size of California) do not obediently restrict their impact to the boundaries of Brazil, Peru, and Colombia.

Seemingly a world apart, about 4,500 miles, lies the Sierra Nevada snowpack that irrigates 7,000,000 acres of fruit, vegetables, and nut production in California's Central Valley. Climate scientists have warned that it may become threatened with drought caused by guess what? – the disappearing Amazon.

We are connected to each other in ways that we understand and in ways that we cannot yet comprehend. What happens in Brazil, where 60% of the Amazon lies, impacts our food security, our way of life and life itself. The scale of interaction and impact is the whole Earth – its climate, biodiversity, ocean currents and salinity, freshwater availability, and sea-level rise.

The scale of climate change activism must also reflect the global systemic nature of our living Earth. Dividing our actions/activism into parts and pieces limits us to un-sustained moments of impact and yields, and, as *The Guardian Newspaper* signatories bemoaned in 2019, *"insufficient urgency to meet the climate crisis."*

So, to answer Bill McKibben's essential question asked on the cover of his book *FALTER – Has the Human Game Begun to Play Itself Out?*

The answer is "yes."

The War

Not a politically correct metaphor, but the right one.

Can war be non-violent? Yes.

Imagine if every major environmental organization across the globe embodied the spirit of dividing, conquering, and collaborating, and chose one of those 200 crisis points from the "A" list and one or two from the "B" list and several from "C."

Imagine if each one of these primary organizations is allied with other environmental initiatives that are smaller with fewer resources and are more local. And then another tier of alliance and another until there is a diverse community of players dedicated and designated for each hot spot.

Each crisis point would become a battle front with a dynamic leadership team all-in to win. And we the people across the globe will be the soldiers, the financiers, the protesters, the volunteers, the artists, the journalists – and when and wherever possible, the voters.

Together, we will move the climate change and ecological activism paradigm from an individual sport to a team sport to a championship league to a global army. And we fight.

Victory is de-carbonizing and re-wilding at scale.

It's simple.

But it isn't.

Chapter 8: But it isn't

Adding to the presumed "impossibility" of these Climate Activist Movement (CAM) ideas are two undermining dynamics that stifle the forward movement of ecological restoration and climate repair.

First, many people assume that to meet the climate crisis they must virtually disappear. Cars are taboo. Planes are the enemy. Consumerism is antithetical to ecological preservation. An autoimmune response of sort happens, and we attack ourselves for just being. This dynamic can be crippling if not paralyzing. It contributes to despair, cynicism, and reinforces the tendency to do nothing, to sit on the sidelines and keep things unchanged. It empowers inertia.

Second, if I am an autoworker, a lawnmower manufacturer, a coal miner, flight attendant or a palm oil plantation worker, what happens to my future? Am I left in the dust, scorned, and forgotten? What happens to my community? What happens to the fabric of my life?

How livable is a future that is as disrupted as climate change activism appears to demand? Is that future car-less? Is there less freedom to enjoy life? Does it mean going backwards? Do avocadoes in the Northeast U.S. become a fond memory for those who remember the time before the "Climate Woke War?"

These prospects threaten to deny us our modernity; steal our freedoms; condemn us to hypocrisy and guilt; and strip, from many, their place in the world, particularly their economic security.

These are not hopeful prospects.

How do we sort through these conundrums?

Humanity will have an environmental impact on this Earth. That is an undeniable fact. But that impact is not by definition a stab in the back or to the heart of our planet. You are not "bad" for just being. We must dispel this notion for anyone who is carrying that burden and push back against those who are leveraging that notion to engender scare tactics that discourage climate action.

The Earth is resilient. CO2, the atmospheric gas we primarily attribute to climate change is natural. Plants and animals need it. Our respiration releases CO2 with every breath. The oceans absorb it. Forestlands store it. Stable CO2 levels have played a valuable role in keeping the Earth warmish, but not too warm.

What we have today is no secret. It is a double whammy of our own making – a fossil fuels addiction that has created a glut of greenhouse gases like carbon dioxide in tandem with an assault on global ecosystems like rainforests, peatlands and grasslands that naturally store carbon.

The fix is also no secret. We need to burn less fossil fuel (a lot less) and we need to conserve and re-wild like crazy. And then hope we've done enough to slow down global warming.

But in any fix scenario that I can imagine, success will not look like five climate-change steps forward and zero back. It will not look like you and me never driving or flying again. It will not be a world without supermarket oranges and avocadoes in northern climes. There will be hamburgers.

How about starting right now with five steps forward and two back – a net gain of three?

Five Forward

We have to declare how to move forward, even in the face of overwhelming obstacles. Why? Because the movement that comes alive within this *Climate Emergency Plan* is more powerful than both the billionaire class and its narrow self-interests and the ruling political class of climate skeptics and deniers now taking root as the Trump administration establishes itself.

The transformative power that lives within the movement envisioned here is hard to see through the dense fog that separates us from our shared longings for responsible stewardship and that obscures our human potential for what is possible.

I refer back to Nobel Prize winning Ilya Prigogine's keen observation.

"When a complex system is far from equilibrium, small islands of coherence in a sea of chaos have the capacity to shift the entire system to a higher order."

We can be the small islands of coherence. Believe it!

We move forward.

How about an across the globe Marshall Plan-like commitment to fast-track green urban transport and reduce, if not eliminate the single largest source of transportation-related fossil fuel emissions?

How about a Green New Deal-like commitment here in the U.S. to connect the largest urban areas within 600 hundred miles of each other with super-high-speed rail or hyperloop-type routes? And in turn significantly reduce short-trip air travel and the related atmospheric pollution it causes.

How about establishing mandatory carbon sequestration rules reflecting the real costs and the real responsibilities for every kind of travel and living?

How about re-directing exponentially more investment dollars to advancing solar, wind, geothermal and tidal technologies, electrical grid-scale batteries, hydrogen fuel applications, green concrete, aviation efficiencies, alternative refrigerants and much more?

How about an immediate focus on overhauling the lawnmower and recreational vehicle industries that account for more than 5% of the air pollution in the U.S.? Running one gas lawnmower for one hour is equivalent in air pollution impact to running 11 new cars for an hour. Add the pollution from gasoline-powered weed wackers and leaf blowers and you have an important piece of our 21rst century living that needs to urgently change.

For anyone who might now be lurching towards a fit of apoplexy at the prospect of their beloved lawnmower being taken away, I have four things to say.

First, I love lawnmowing.

Second, there will be lawnmowing in the future, but there needs to be as few internal combustion lawnmowers as possible. That's the challenge. We should be aiming for zero.

Third, with such sea-changes needed to be made in our "ordinary" lives comes the understanding that there are businesses and livelihoods and futures that are all married to the affected industries. This impact must be anticipated and met with both an urgent and sensible transition plan.

Four, procrastinating and delaying these necessary changes to de-carbonize is not an option.

There will be disruptions. There will be tough moments. There will be sacrifices. There are uncertainties.

And there is this indisputable fact.

There is a future Earth that we in the present are responsible for, and we should do our best to protect it for our children and theirs and theirs.

Two Back

There is no magic wand in sight to align the world with magical/enlightened thinking, even mine. We will not always go forward. We will continue to generate CO2, but how much will we reduce it and how much will we sequester with re-wilding?

5,000,000 acres or about 8000 square miles of primary Amazon Rain Forest, the so called "lungs" of our planet, were lost in 2020. That's 10X the size of Maui in one year or about the size of Vermont if you like. Way too much! 600,000 of those acres were from fires that scorched the Chiquitano tropical forest in Bolivia

The numbers are numbing. The scale is hard to wrap your brain around and the fix is incomprehensible. Where does the tipping point lie when the Amazon biome no longer produces enough rainfall to support its ecosystems? The answer is debatable. But what is fact is that point in time is getting closer and closer to now. What is fact is that we are in a race, actually a battle, to protect this treasure and vital organ of our planet and hopefully push that timeframe back.....to never.

What do we do?

How about half of us focus on championing the five steps forward (make it 6) and half of us focus on reducing the two steps backwards (make it 1 ½)?

On the one-hand such a simplistic notion seems like an unrealizable, stupid abstraction, if not insane. On the other, it makes perfect sense.

So, what do we do? Ignore what makes perfect sense or dismiss it because it's impossible?

You know where I stand. We pick up the ball of string labeled "Climate Activist Movement," find the loose end and follow it because we know it is the right thing to try to do.

Chapter 9: The Money

Let's dispel one rebuttal to what's possible – there isn't the money.

Yeah, there is.

There are so many ways to look at this.

How about reversing the $1.5 trillion-dollar tax cut give-away (that went into effect in 2018) to corporations and the wealthiest and put that money into the green urban transport piggy-bank and accelerate that work 100-fold? Although Trump 2.0 will not allow this, Trump 2.0 will not last forever.

How about wrapping your brain around the fact that we Americans consume 140 billion gallons of gasoline annually? Our airlines use 18 billion gallons of aviation fuel. We burn 5 billion gallons of heating oil. We use 27.5 trillion cubic feet of natural gas. And in 2018, American coal weighed in at 691 million tons.

That's a lot of CO_2. In fact, we represent 4.34% of the world's population yet produce almost 14% of its fossil fuel CO_2 emission.

Rather than just feeling victimized by this incongruity as in… *"WTF can I do?"* …. we need to respond to what we know is problematic (i.e. excessive reliance on fossil fuels) and find ways to also make this indisputable problem work for us on behalf of the future.

How?

Go bold! Tax it for starters.

And use that money to transform our nation's infrastructure. Restore Midwest grasslands. Re-forest everywhere possible. Make our agriculture production regenerative and more climate friendly. Invest in "green "technologies. Incentivize "green" every-day living. Solarize intensively. Re-explore small scale modular nuclear reactors. There is so much we can do if we galvanize our will to do so.

But isn't a more "tax It" strategy a non-starter – political suicide – sacrilege?

Yes, definitely all three, if the boogey-man cards that scare and confuse people are allowed to be played unchallenged.

It is so easy to default to why something cannot work. "Congress will never allow it." "The billionaire class will kill it." "The inflation will be a disaster." And on and on. This is the So-So force at work. It does not have the capacity to recognize an "Island of Coherence" and its import unless it was a tropical vacation destination.

Remember, we are in a Pearl Harbor-like moment, possibly X 100 or a 1,000,000. We need to find new ways to move forward and prove that we are a multi-generational "can do" populace rather than offer more of the same stale excuses to stay stupid and prove that we are not.

Taxes are not monolithically bad. Yes, they fund way too much unnecessary waste. They subsidize industries that should not have that benefit. Unquestionably, they can be regressive and unfair and hurt those with less financial means. And yes, they can be plain stupid. The obvious point is that there is room for improvement, a lot of room. But the most important point here is a call to action, your action. Vote to identify and oppose waste. Vote to fix our tax policies. Make government work even if conventional wisdom declares such notions to be naive and fanciful.

Invest in the stability of the future.

And don't forget.

There is also a flip side to the idea of a "tax" which needs to see the light of day. In that light, taxes are potentially more than just a burden to bear and resent. They are also tools to harness and express our collective intention and power. They have a purpose. They have potential. They can be justified.

When we add compost to the soil to increase its fertility, that compost has a cost. Think of it as a tax, but it is really an investment, and the benefits are astronomical. That "tax" feeds us today. That "tax" will feed the future tomorrow. Without paying for that fertility and investing in the soil, we would be doing little more than mining and eventually depleting it.

Similarly, without taxing carbon and investing in the "fertility" and the stability of the future, we are robbing it; we are depleting it; we are dooming it.

So, when those boogey-man cards are played, as they always are, by those fear mongers invested in the status quo, we can say to them, "Hell no" to our tax dollars supporting government waste, duplicative bureaucracies, unnecessary military programs, and insane cost overruns. And "Hell yes" to fighting climate change, re-wilding and investing in the greenest future possible.

Am I being naïve? Yes, if we are just cacophonous voices ineffectually (as we presently are) demanding sanity. Absolutely not, if the Revolution in Activism being championed here begins.

We need to tax carbon smartly, justly and spend every dollar wisely. And we need to reject straight-out the poverty mentality that there is no money.

Because if that were true, how did we find $1.7 trillion dollars so the F-35 fighter jet could have its future? Yet somehow, we can't find the money for our children to have theirs.

All that said and despite what appears, post-election 2024, to be insanity moving back into the driver's seat of our American lives, taxes are an aside. The Climate Activist Movement (CAM) and the *PARALLEL* Economy do not constellate around tax policy.

Chapter 10: Manifesting Brute Cash

There is no escape from the reality of money. Climate change activism and ecological restoration need cash and lots of it to finance de-carbonizing and re-wilding. Being a poor cash-strapped movement is not an option any longer. It cannot be an excuse for inaction, half-measures, or failure.

Government cannot do it all, but it can do a lot. To reiterate, it needs to fulfill its critical role in overhauling an unjust and wasteful tax system. It needs to legislate key policies like "smart" carbon taxation and appropriate funding to champion initiatives like the *Green New Deal* or something like it and even better. It needs to institute progressive regulations that rapidly advance de-carbonizing. The U.S. government needs to lead by example across the globe.

Setbacks are inevitable. Obviously, barring the unforeseen, the second Trump presidency will not deliver that leadership. Yes, a setback. But waiting for political leadership, in any case, is not an IMPACT strategy and does not drive the "Revolution" envisioned here.

Even if the above tax enlightenment and re-prioritizations were to magically manifest, the climate revolution we need is going to take a lot more oomph and engagement than our government or any government can manifest – a lot more.

It needs to be, first and foremost, a from the bottom-up world-wide people's movement that showcases the spine, the will, and the urgency that politicians and bureaucracies, most often, can only react to rather than create.

We can all plainly see the fickleness of governing in the United States by Executive Order where actions and policies have the impermanence of tumbleweeds blowing hard right and left from one administration to the other.

Hence, one of the essential ingredients needed to both push forward with that urgency and be more independent from the vagaries of those tumbleweeds is what I call "brute cash" – the cash to do everything and anything to turn the tide, in haste, on global warming.

Think of it as "the people's cash." There cannot be too much of this kind of financial muscle.

This muscle can have a lot of different looks.

Look #1, for example, is the emergence of the *Wyss Campaign for Nature*, a special project of the Wyss Foundation that aims to conserve and protect 30% of the planet's lands and oceans by 2030. Backed up by a $1.5 billion investment and in collaboration with the National Geographic Society, The Nature Conservancy and many local partners, nine projects in 13 countries will receive, as a starter project, $48 million in assistance. The size of the far-reaching areas to receive this promising benefit is about 10,000,000 acres of land (about the size of Switzerland) and 17,000 square kilometers (6563 sq. miles) of ocean. The countries affected are Argentina, Zimbabwe, Australia, Costa Rica, Romania, the Andes Amazon region and the Caribbean Marine Protected Areas.

Hopefully, this is just the beginning of the flexing of this kind of philanthropic muscle.

What could be done with $10 billion or a $trillion? That's the way we need to think and that's the kind of money we need to manifest. And I believe it is possible.

Consider the potential of Look #2. In 1985, 1.9 billion people watched the "Live Aid" concert for Ethiopian famine relief. Freddie Mercury and Queen were one of the highlights. Approximately $127,000,000 dollars (history.com/this-day-in-history/live-aid-concert) was raised through that action. In today's dollars that is $322,000,000.

More than 3.5 billion watched the 2016 Rio Summer Olympics; 2 billion watched the funeral of Princess Diana in 1997; 2 billion were on-hand for the memorial service for Michael Jackson in 2009 (Beyond the Dash Blog, April 3, 2019); 1.9 billion watched the wedding of Prince Harry and Meghan Markle (The Economic Times (ET), May 20, 2018).

How much money could be raised in our interconnected world today in a united climate activism campaign? Imagine again those big, coordinated waves of celebrity, children, musicians, unified environmental organizations, and the many others that were listed above. Imagine the 2026 – 28 – 30 – 32 Olympics all tied into the Global Climate Change movement and planning for it right now. Imagine the billions of people watching FIFA World Cup Soccer every four years also becoming engaged as part of this movement.

Why not? What is standing in the way? Is it the "impossible" again?

Chapter 11: What is standing in the way?

The climate deniers, the resistors, and those firmly entrenched on the wrong side of history will not come to their senses in time, if ever. Despite an "All are Welcome" invitation, Kumbaya will likely remain a fiction in this Climate Activist Movement and *PARALLEL* Economy conception.

The reaction to the *Green New Deal (GND) Resolution* introduced in 2019 by Senator Ed Markey of Massachusetts and Representative Alexandria Ocasio Cortez of New York illustrates this. The Resolution should, in principle, be a no-brainer. De-carbonize as fast as possible. Champion economic and social justice. And protect and care for people who will be most impacted by the transitional upheavals as we move away from fossil fuels.

Setting aside any arguable weaknesses and deficiencies in the Deal, in spirit, what could the problem possibly be?

<u>One of the Battle Lines</u>

One battleline constellates around the following assertion. *The Green New Deal* (GND) is a destructive, socialist daydream and will be a massive government take-over. Donald Trump claimed it would take away "your airplane rights." Senator Tom Cotton of Arkansas declared "the proposal would confiscate cars." (Feb. 21, 2019, NY Times, Lisa Friedman).

We should all get use to this "socialism" scare tactic. No doubt the word has been focus grouped to death. It's a very effective weapon because it is so easy to apply. Just the mere mention of the word casts the dark shadow of government control. One of the intended links is, of course, to communism. People naturally fear and reject such a prospect, whether it is unfounded or not.

In fact, *The Green New Deal* has zip to do with "socialism" in the pejorative sense. The link is a total red herring (no pun intended), but it works to evoke fear and distrust. It closes minds. Rather than being, at long last, a breath of fresh air and hopeful leadership, the *GND* resolution becomes a threatening evil prospect. A battle line is clearly drawn here, and those championing de-carbonizing and rewilding better be prepared to put the socialism, democratic socialism (and communism) labels to sleep.

The *Green New Deal* is not a mutant. It is not anti-business, but rather pro-innovation and responsible and responsive leadership. When the resolution is fleshed out, there will no doubt be plenty to debate. But what is certain is that the *GND* is striving to meet the world ethically, responsibly, and positively.

Notably, what is mutant is a sweeping battle plan to dismantle key environmental protections (and much more) – Project 2025. Published in 2022 by the Heritage Foundation, this initiative would cause, according to the Sierra Club, everything from rules to curb hazardous air pollutants to programs that help make cleaner and more energy efficient purchases more affordable to be on the chopping block. Agencies like the EPA and National Oceanic and Atmospheric Administration (NOAA) would be gutted. Peer-reviewed science would be sidelined, and polluters' economic interests would be prioritized in government decision-making.

What is standing in the way? It is our complex and often confounding human nature because the above paragraph contradicts sensibility and responsible adulthood. What else could explain the rejection of climate science and the undermining of environmental regulations?

Let me answer that – the war of information and facts. Where do we get our news? How do we discern what is fake? How does and how will Artificial Intelligence (AI) and foreign government interventions drive conspiracies and erode our self-preservation human sensibility and divert us from responsible adulthood?

A variation of a Turkish proverb goes something like this.

"The forest was shrinking, but the trees kept voting for the Axe, for the Axe was clever and convinced the trees that his handle was made of wood, he was one of them."

The "Axe" is arguably now President Donald Trump. Project 2025 will move to the foreground. "We" become more important than ever. Maybe the levers of power are in different hands than many of us despondingly think. Maybe those levers are, as I believe, potentially in our hands. Not entirely, but in ways that we have not realized.

A world without McDonald's and Ben & Jerry's?

Another corrosive battle line is a scare tactic that ominously declared that the *Green New Deal* would cause the number of cows in the U.S. to go from 94,000,000 to zero. Translation – the end of hamburgers and ice cream and the beginning of the apocalypse. This is, of course, nonsense. But can you think of anything more galvanizing to turn public opinion against you than the prospect of a hamburger and ice cream-less world, a world without McDonalds and Ben & Jerry's?

It is a fact that farming practices can be destructive. Industrial scale feedlots; pesticide use; agricultural run-off into streams, rivers, and lakes; antibiotic over-use; and excess tilling are all problematic. But farming can also be restorative. The Regenerative Agriculture model can help to reverse climate change by rebuilding soil fertility, minimizing tillage, and sequestering carbon.

Rather than fearing a world without hamburgers and Ice cream, we should direct our focus to the real threat facing us – Project 2025 and the end of environmental regulations.

Chapter 12: Down the Rabbit Hole

Part of the cynicism that greets me when I talk to others about my climate activism ideas is rooted in the disheartening contempt for our capitalist economic system. The gist is "there is no hope for the Earth as long as profit-making drives our everyday lives."

This argument has legs, but it is also complicated. We shouldn't fall into oppositional camps without at least understanding each other.

For example, Arizona, one of the sunniest places in the U.S. gets only 10% of its energy from the sun (2023), but also 10% from coal (2023). Why? Let's go all the way down the rabbit hole with this one to see if there is a bottom and to also better understand each other.

One argument makes the case that the State's biggest utility, Arizona Public Service (APS), a subsidiary of the publicly traded Pinnacle West Capital Corporation has historically opposed solar. Why? Because the for-profit driven Pinnacle West has other important investments in nuclear energy and fossil fuel generation, and solar power has potentially represented a threat to their profit-making plans for the present and the future.

But this reduction is incomplete and not fair.

Counter to the above, Pinnacle West is, in fact, investing in solar energy with 100 megawatts planned by 2025. Additionally, 850 megawatts of large-scale battery storage are in the queue to meet future demand when energy usage peaks, particularly after the sun sets. That's 950 megawatts of new clean energy technology.

So, we can't simply drop Pinnacle West in "the climate be damned" capitalist corporation box.

But counter to the counter is also consideration of the 2018 ballot initiative, Proposition 127, that would have amended Arizona's state constitution to require electric utilities to use renewable energy for 50% of their power by 2035.

Although this initiative is somewhat historical now in early 2025, Pinnacle West actively supported Arizona's Prop 127 public defeat. Here was arguably a big chance to take a big renewable leap forward into the future. And chances are all we get in this war of climate action to meet the global warming crisis. There are no happy-ending guarantees. Maybe we should put Pinnacle West in that business-as-usual box after all?

Perhaps, but not yet. It is so easy to be tribal. We're the good climate friendly guys. They're the bad corporate greedy guys.

Prop 127's intended 50% renewable target also had an Achilles heel that left it not only vulnerable to attack and defeat, but also with valid public concerns. What would the cost impact be to consumers to reach that 50% target given the many subsequent demands on APS to maneuver its energy assets to meet what would have been a constitutionally mandated action?

It is right here where our rabbit hole drops precipitously into darkness.

Opponents of Prop 127, like APS, exploited the uncertainties of these cost repercussions to its customers. This was easily done because consumers carry the actual costs of the grid and the operations. And nothing galvanizes resistance to change by consumers more than pocket-book issues.

The real cost impacts of Prop 127 were arguably unknown. For example, would meeting the constitutional mandate have required APS to prematurely offload costly assets such as its Palo Verde nuclear generating station in Maricopa County? And with what consequences and costs to consumers who would have to ultimately foot the bill? APS and its allies leveraged this scary uncertainty.

Looking back at Prop 127 in 2018 and now looking ahead, who should do this analysis and answer consequential questions that will either make or break the momentum to de-carbonize or make or break the economic viability of a utility that in turn might drive the cost of power to consumers through the roof? Without a definitive answer in real time to these complex questions, the Prop 127 vote was subject to politics, big money, and polarizing rhetoric on both sides of the divide. It was defeated and so perhaps was climate action on a scale and in a timeframe that would have set an example for the rest of the country.

In this darkness of not knowing the consequences of big change, who should be trusted? The Pinnacle West Capital boardroom whose fiduciary responsibilities likely guarantee that profit-making is paramount? Or the climate scientists and activists trying to prevent or at least forestall the failing of our planetary life support systems?

This is the dance we are faced with to collectively learn how to do. Business-as-usual will sink us. This is a given. But climate advocacy absent embracing the realities of business interests and public impact will thwart progress and sink us as well.

If the 50% renewable target is not a "wouldn't it be nice," but a must to advance de-carbonization then three things must follow.

Consumers should not be scared into being short-sighted and voting against what the science is telling us needs to happen.

The real costs to implement changes that are a "must" need to be mediated within a mindset or collaborative culture that transcends "us against them" but rather "us for us."

In order for such a collaborative culture to emerge, there needs to be a safety net plan to protect both the interests of the consumer and the utility or business interest.

Such a collaborative culture may seem impossible, like expecting water and oil to mix. But oil and water can mix and do mix every day in real life courtesy of emulsifiers. The interests of Arizona Public Service, consumers, and climate activists can mix if each chooses to reasonably consider the other; if each agrees not to condemn the other, but to be suspended together in a working agreement – a miracle of sorts.

Arizona's Prop 127 was right in its objective to hasten the use of renewable energy. And its Achilles heel should have been met not with resistance, but with creative and groundbreaking problem solving. Anything less amounts to tired excuses hailing from an aging economic paradigm that no longer works for planet Earth and its residents.

Prop 127 was a defeat for all of us on the planet. The organizers need to pass along the lessons they learned. Because the next battle is somewhere else tomorrow and the day after and the day after that. We cannot afford to reinvent the wheel each time. We need to leverage this failure and all others to plan for future successes.

And no matter what, there is no way that 10% or 20% of power from renewables in Arizona is okay. We must be much smarter tactically, more resilient, more strategically financed and we have to be ready to push back hard against business-as-usual, while not autonomically demonizing and rejecting business-people, their concerns, and their interests.

As such, "The War" that I referenced is not against those engaged in collaborative problem solving and compromise – five forward, two back. But it is against people who are all-in to impose their ideologies and win for themselves at all costs, even the climate, even our democracy. Project 2025 is the poster-child for this narcissistic ethos.

Does capitalism doom us?

Many will answer "Yes," but not me. Capitalism does not doom us to outcomes or expressions of greed, amoralism and environmental catastrophe, in much the same way that many genetic mutations do not doom us to contract any given disease. It is possible, perhaps in some situations probable, but not a fait accompli.

This analogy may seem a stretch, but it is instructive.

The field of epigenetics considers genes and their expression, that is, why and why not some genes express themselves in any given individual. For example, 45% of women with the BRCA 2 gene mutation will develop breast cancer by age 70. This is obviously a significant and concerning percentage, but my point here is that the majority of women will be okay despite the mutation.

Similarly, the predisposition to thoughtless opportunism in order to make a buck may be a problematic capitalist behavior, but not necessarily. There are other variables that influence the kind of expression we see.

Unfortunately, in both cases, epigenetics and capitalism, it is not known exactly what turns on or off a gene to manifest any given disease or what misleads a mind to make or not make abhorrent and immoral choices for the sake of personal gain and financial profit.

But what is clear is that human behavior can corrupt any economic system or any presenting situation. In the case of capitalism, there is a broad range of degrees of behavior possible, from outright evil such as ivory poaching to Certified B Corporations that are dedicated to using business activity as a force of good.

The *PARALLEL* Economy aims to be one of those forces of good despite the economic system that it may be classified to be functioning within.

The tendency to reduce complexities like genetics and entire economic systems to certainties reflects either ignorance, misguided assumptions, or entrenched hopelessness. Whatever the reason, it does not serve the greater good because feeling doomed and powerless makes the present disappear. And in life it is the present and what we try to do within it that counts the most.

Post-script and a reminder

The 2018 Arizona ballot initiative was a two-steps backward moment, no matter what side of the fence you were on – for or against. Actually, the illusion is that there are two sides to this fence, because dividing is after all what fences do and that is what we expect. But not this one. When it comes to planetary life support systems, there may be fences but there is no divide. There is only one side, the one we are all living on together. Case in point is the cataclysmic Los Angeles fires in early 2025. Everything burns, rich and poor, black and white, Democrat and Republican.

There was also good news and big steps forward that soon followed in Arizona. The Navajo Generating Station near Page, Arizona, one of the nation's largest coal plants and polluters, shut down in 2019. And that generating capacity is now being replaced with cleaner natural gas from other power plants (Mesquite and Gila River) and solar arrays and battery storage. Remember, five forward – two back.

The journey to the impossible that will not fail us does not rest on perfection and purity, but on our growing into a movement of empowered community and collaboration.

Chapter 13: A brief return to hamburgers

It may be true that the most expedient way to make money in the world of beef cows and hamburgers is through industrial scale feedlots.

But that cost efficient and profit-making production system is accelerating the depletion of carbon stores and increasing atmospheric methane and nitrous oxide. And on top of that, feedlots increase the likelihood of water pollution due to agriculture run-off from unvegetated ground and increase the risk of creating antibiotic resistant strains of bacteria due to a production system that relies on the over-use of antibiotics to be successful.

What is the real cost of accelerating the production of global warming gases like CO_2, NO_2 and methane to humanity as a whole? What is the real cost of water pollution? What is the real cost of reducing the effectiveness of antibiotics to each and every one of us? And are any of these incremental costs factored into the real cost of beef production?

The answer is no. If they were, (I bet) feedlots would not be the most expedient way to make money in the world of beef?

There needs to be a reckoning here and in turn a disruption of business-as-usual. Feedlots and Concentrated Area Feeding Operations (CAFOS) where a 1000 or more cows are confined for 45 days or more in an area without vegetation need to be phased out.

Will capitalist behavior allow for this and support a transition to a regenerative agriculture model? Are we confronted with an inevitability that it will not; that no one is going to voluntarily surrender their right to cheap hamburgers, the climate and the environment be damned?

There is no "inevitability" to our human behavior. What is certain is our human potential for glorious triumph or abject failure and everything in between.

The end of capitalism is not a pre-condition for accelerated re-wilding and de-carbonizing. The end is certainly not necessary to build and finance the

Climate Activist Movement. And its demise is an unnecessary demand in order for us to stop our "faltering."

PART 4

More on the *PARALLEL* Economy

Chapter 14: The First Toehold

What gives me any sense of optimism that the collective "we" can ever become the powerful?

I believe in our human potential.

Yes, that potential creates draconian impulses like Project 2025. That potential rejects the Chevron Deference doctrine, a foundational Supreme Court precedent, which served for 40+ years as a means to empower federal agencies like the EPA and the USDA to issue pesticide restrictions and food safety regulations. That potential is horrifyingly expressing itself today in Israel and Gaza.

But that potential can also be miraculous in its generosity, its creativity, its unselfishness, its capacity to mobilize and unify, its expressions of beauty, and its determination.

How do we choose? How will we choose?

Becoming the powerful to champion rewilding and decarbonizing is a possibility, not a probability.

The incarnation of the *PARALLEL* Economy will take a village. Villages exist, albeit imperfectly. Human collaboration and cooperation on behalf of shared values and objectives is not a fantastical impulse born of my imagination. Human evolution has already advanced this far.

You may recall that Bill McKibben wrote in *FALTER* that "we have the tools to stand up to the powerful and reckless." And my response was and remains – the *PARALLEL* Economy and the Climate Activist Movement set out with an additional objective – to become the powerful. We also have the tools to do this. This is the only way. But how do we do that?

We become the powerful by giving that possibility a chance. It is that simple and so far, we have not done that adequately.

The *PARALLEL* Economy will start with a pool of several billion dollars.

Yes, Billions. Maybe this starting point is too big of a bite. Crazy, in a word. Maybe. But on the other hand, maybe this reticence is conventional thinking, or the wisdom gleaned from and relevant to an ordinary entrepreneurial life but not to a global crisis heading towards calamity.

I am looking for the beeline to results. Realistically, I think established institutions will shy away from the *PARALLEL* Economy conception. The ideas are too big and unwieldy. Its not-for-profit orientation casts a shadow on creating a viable capitalization strategy.

I can hear the refrain (and to date myself) from the 1989 Kevin Costner movie, Field of Dreams, *Build it and they will come*. I think this is true of the *PARALLEL* Economy. Something must be built that captures the possibility I am envisioning in real time and real life. And then they will come.

Where does the capital come from to start a bank, a lending program, and a credit card? Not in the ordinary way unless the *PARALLEL* Economy vision is embraced/incorporated by the likes of the Climate First Bank, Amalgamated Bank, and/or Forbright Bank. That could happen. I would welcome it but let us set that hopeful possibility aside and consider what "not in the ordinary way" might look like.

The *Climate Emergency Plan* and its two components, the *PARALLEL* Economy and the Climate Activist Movement (CAM) will start with a pool of several billion dollars sourced from philanthropic contributions. This money will come together for three reasons or as a result of satisfying three conditions.

1. A knock-your-socks-off management core hovering for the opportunity of a lifetime.
2. Buy-in from the inner circle of climate change activists like Bill McKibben.
3. Hollywood and/or celebrity engagement and endorsement.

The knock-your-socks-off management core is out there. It doesn't have to be invented. The banking, financial and management expertise is ready. Who could disagree with that? So, that's not impossible.

Climate-centric credit cards exist. Environmentally committed Certified B Corp banks like the Climate First Bank exist. Influential activists like Bill McKibben are keenly aware of the importance of banking institutions.

In fact, in a February 18, 2020 email to me, Bill wrote, in response to my *Climate Emergency Credit Card* idea – *"This strikes me as a fascinating idea."*

Buy-in from the inner circle of climate change activists like Bill McKibben is a reasonable assumption. Definitely possible.

Celebrity engagement is an established universe. Who could disagree with that? From Jerry Lewis who raised almost $2.5 billion for the Muscular Dystrophy Association over the years; to Oprah Winfrey's high-profile influence and charitable clout; to global music extravaganzas such as the Concert for Bangladesh and athletic charitable events like the London Marathon that raised over $90 million in 2019, celebrity engagement on a massive global scale for climate action is just a matter of time. What it is waiting for is the *Climate Emergency Plan* coming to light in these pages to engage its focus and rally around.

So, we don't have an impossible problem. Let us put that notion to rest.

And here is something else we can put to rest. I threw out *"The Climate Emergency Plan will start with "several billion dollars"* not because that has to be the starting point. Not at all. But perhaps that kind of capitalization should be entertained, if not the starting point. And if so, my point is that it is not impossible, and we should be open to it.

<u>Brain-Dead Sloths</u>

If we do not open ourselves up to a new era of flexible thinking now that responds to the appropriate amount of urgency we are facing, then climate change will be the human story of the future. And we will be the brain-dead sloths that no one in that future will understand because our choices and degree of failure will be incomprehensible to them. This is very possible.

There is not a "you" and "me" kind of divide in this global warming crisis. Yes, there are climate crisis deniers. Yes, I may have disdain for the pollution caused by the burning of coal, but not for the coal miners or the millions of people doing their best to cook and stay warm. Yes, there are profound and consequential economic injustices that must be addressed. Yet in the grand scheme of almost eight billion people living their lives here on the planet surface, there is only "we."

As one of those eight billion, I have an oil furnace, a heat pump, and a wood stove in my home. I am not above it all. I am both the problem, and I want to be part of the solution. To do this, I need help. The *PARALLEL* Economy and Climate Activist Movement imaginations are an important piece of that help which is why I am trying to champion them here.

The underlying ethos to invite everyone to be a part of the solution is not a business strategy, it is a survival response. It is the way to act when the only house on the planet – our house - is on fire.

Here is something else that should be factored into the impossibility equation. A *Climate Emergency Bank,* lending program, and credit card are actually homerun business ideas to any open-minded, discerning pair of eyes. And by design and purpose, its "profits" will solely benefit climate action.

Aren't there enough of us weary of the plunder of Wall Street and the other global exchanges ravaging Planet Earth? Aren't there enough of us sitting on the sidelines feeling hopeless, powerless, cynical, ambivalent, and checked-out on the subject?

The *Climate Emergency Plan* opens a door that has been invisible. That door is an opening to being connected to a movement to meet an impending crisis that does not require yet another donation or membership. Most of us use credit cards and/or contactless transaction services. We all use banks. Many of us need to borrow. Why not do it all safely and securely within a *PARALLEL* Economic world with its climate focus and dedication? Is this an impossible toehold? It should not be.

Chapter 15: More on Philanthropy

I have suggested utilizing a pool of several billion dollars derived from philanthropy to create a toehold to get the *Climate Emergency Plan* started.

I believe, so far, that this approach must be the way. Terms such as investing, ownership, return on investment and exit strategies fall away in this visioning. Even B Corps, albeit with their many admirable socially responsible principles, are subject to the distractions and side-shows caused by the profit-making motive.

Not-for-profits are also subject to being compromised and diminished. Some not-for-profit CEOs make in excess of $1 million. The "slippery slope virus" exists within each of us and hence potentially in all human endeavor. But if we are taking bets, I will bet on the not-for-profit or the cooperative economic model for a *PARALLEL* Economic life.

Remember, I am not pouring cement. I am throwing out thoughts and leanings. Maybe the B Corp model is, at the end of the day, perfect.

Imagine a philanthropy sector that becomes foundational to the manifestation of a *PARALLEL* economy. I am not suggesting that philanthropy become the singular fuel for *PARALLEL*. That would be foolish. Rather, I am imagining that philanthropy could be used to "prime the pump" to get something started.

Philanthropy could function both as a source of high-risk capital or it could be leveraged to make higher risk lending more viable by serving to relieve the perceived risks that cause traditional lenders to turn down prospective borrowers.

I see philanthropy and low interest lending as the bridge to self-sustaining cash flow in a *PARALLEL* Economic and CAM world. Also, philanthropy would be the power behind aspirational "can and must-dos" that are understood to be high risk, when convention cannot rise above "can't do."

There is nothing revolutionary or magical in this thinking. For example, in September 2021, the Hewlett Foundation launched the not-for-profit

Climate Finance Fund, a philanthropic platform that helps to mobilize capital for climate solutions. Marilyn Waite, who leads the *Climate Finance Fund* reflects in her writing that there is a funding problem for innovative ideas because of the conservative nature of bank lending and the difficulties of attracting investment capital to high-risk entrepreneurial initiatives. The place called the "Valley of Death" otherwise known to me as the business graveyard, is a term that Marilyn has used to describe the consequential failed launches and business failures when funding evaporates or never appears.

The point being is that philanthropy is a frontier that is not far out on Cloud 9. It is right in front of us, and we need to creatively parlay it right now with abandon. Serving as a risk mediator, philanthropy is what will underlie the delivery of the *Climate Emergency Plan* and its transformative potential to meet the global warming crisis.

Americans charitably gave $499 billion dollar in 2022. Corporate giving reached $21 billion, and Foundations contributed about $105 billion – more than $620 billion in total. In Europe, foundations donated an estimated $60 billion euros to charitable organizations across the European Union.

In addition to traditional philanthropy, there is simply a lot of money floating around that could be applied to incarnating a grand idea such as a competitive *PARALLEL* economic reality. Michael Bloomberg spent around $1 billion on his 2020 presidential campaign aspirations. Tom Steyer spent approximately $250 million on his 2020 campaign. The Harris-Walz campaign spent nearly $1.4 billion in its failed 2024 effort. This is the tip of the iceberg (potentially) of available brute cash to break down barriers, open doors, prove concepts, and respond with the necessary urgency to make a difference, if there was only a way to mobilize that potential.

And there is a way, and it does not have to take forever until it is too late. Why not in the twinkling of an eye?

The Metaphorical "Room" and the "Big Boat"

Why not bring together, in a metaphorical room, the powerful, the influencers, the monied, the connected, the communicators and the inspirers who are making a difference yet want to do more because it is needed. Bring together people like Bill McKibben, Paul Hawken, Greta Thunberg, Naomi Klein, Al Gore, John Kerry, Barack and Michelle Obama, Gina McCarthy, Marilyn Waite, Jasper Van Brakel, Oprah Winfrey, Bill Gates, Lady Gaga, Jane Fonda, Tom Steyer, Lebron James, Michael Bloomberg, Meryl Streep, Ted Turner, Beyonce', Ivan Frishberg, Warren Buffet, Andrew Yang, Robert Redford, MacKenzie Scott, Taylor Swift, Laurene Powell Jobs, Amanda Gorman, Lionel Messi, Alice Louise Walton and on and on.

The list of potential people in this metaphorical global room, prominent or not, could fill a book. Why isn't this possible? And what isn't possible with this kind of convergence of human energy, achievement, and consciousness?

But how naïve of me to think that this convergence is possible when probably everyone that I have assembled in that room is bought into and financially depends on that for-profit paradigm I am intending the *PARALLEL* Economy to disrupt. Is this the catch-22 ambush that has been waiting for my Revolutionary dream?

If so.

The End.

But I do not think so.

The *PARALLEL* Economy I am envisioning is not monolithic in its outlook. Everything does not need to become *//*. *PARALLEL* does not take over the world nor does it have to do so to change the world. But I do think it has to pose, at least initially, as a notable presence to get the "big boat's (our capitalist juggernaut) attention and turn it.

Establishing this undeniable presence will be accomplished by the Climate Activist Movement that *PARALLEL* economics will mobilize and support. This movement represents a meaningful slice of the marketplace that has disposable income. The resulting market trends reflecting engaged global warming activism represent waves, currents and winds that will get the "big boat's" attention. The bigger this movement the bigger the waves, currents, and winds.

The *PARALLEL* Economy needs to become a significant and influential force. That force will inspire other entrepreneurs to align with the // ethos and become allied with the spirit of its decarbonizing and re-wilding focus. Part of the job of the *Climate Emergency Plan's* leadership is to facilitate those alliances. In this way there will be plenty of room under the *PARALLEL* Economic tent for for-profit enterprises.

Similarly, the *PARALLEL* movement will also influence the choices and behaviors of the established and self-absorbed capitalist economy. Imagine if the large fast-food corporations helped reverse the deforestation of the Amazon. What a story that would be! What a win! Imagine if these same corporations wielded their influence to demand a climate responsible and cruelty-free paradigm for raising animals.

Well, maybe if *McPARALLELS*™ gets started tomorrow with an extraordinary amount of buzz and grabs some meaningful market share because there is a movement behind it, the above would begin to happen in response.

And these alliances would be promoted. The capitalist juggernaut would begin to morph in the // direction.

Do we need a time machine?

The point is the Catch-22 does not exist. Once the "big boat" starts truly turning in the direction of de-carbonizing and re-wilding, it will not turn back to its old ways without an extraordinary counter force. And I believe that is impossible!

Do we need a time machine that brings us all to 2050 where we learn of hundreds of millions displaced, hundreds of thousands of people dead every year from climate-related disruption, coastal devastation, a weakened Gulf Stream current turning our climate lives on the east coast of North America and Western Europe upside down? You get the drift.

If we all got that grand futuristic tour of the calamity first-hand and could then transport ourselves back to today, would that metaphorical room stay a pipe dream? Would there still be disempowered, chickens with their heads cut-off laments like…. *"Where will the money ever come from? It is too risky."* Would *the Climate Emergency Plan* become a no-brainer and an imperative?

I believe, yes. And if not the ideas I am trying to capture here and in – Part 5 – Living into the Imagination – that is introduced next, then something else that meets the global warming crisis with the impact needed to stop our faltering.

PART 5

Living into the Imagination

Chapter 16: The CLIMATE EMERGENCY CREDIT CARD

Land of Giants

Here are some credit card fun-facts from Bankrate from a December 21, 2023, post.

In 2022, credit cards were the most used payment method in the U.S. accounting for 31% of transactions. 77% of U.S. adults have at least one credit card. The average American makes almost 186 credit card transactions per year and the average household's credit card balance was $6088. In 2022, credit card spending was $5.6 trillion.

The credit card world is a complex landscape dominated by large banks like Citigroup and JP Morgan Chase and major Credit Card Networks like VISA, Mastercard, Discover and American Express.

The scale is huge in every direction that you look. It is a land of giants.

There were 53.8 billion U.S. card transactions in 2023.

Credit card debt as of the first quarter of 2024 for Americans was $1.115 trillion.

The VISA network had the most cards in circulation in 2021, at 363 million (Bureau of Consumer Financial Protection) U.S. cardholders and 4.2 billion worldwide.

The Mastercard network has 273 million cardholders in the U.S. Worldwide, 2.89 billion Master cards are reported.

Chase Bank, as a card issuer, had the largest credit card share in terms of outstanding balances at $154 billion. American Express weighed in at $115 billion of outstanding balances (Bureau of Consumer Financial Protection).

Citigroup and Chase each have more than eighty million cardholders.

This scale is exactly why it is and is not the perfect place for the *PARALLEL* Economy to find a toehold to launch.

It is because credit cards are not an original idea. Most everyone (in developed countries) has at least one. And every merchant accepts them. There is a ready super-highway of know-how and technologies in place to handle all the interfaces between banks and merchants with relative ease. In short, there is no pioneering. There is something instant to plug into that does not have to be created. This is potentially a big plus.

It is not the perfect place to start because banks do not materialize out of thin air nor do millions of cardholders magically hold "your" special card. There is inarguably a chasm between the *PARALLEL* Economy idea and its *Climate Emergency Bank* and the many demanding financial realities and practicalities that are unavoidable.

But there is not a chasm between the *PARALLEL* idea itself and the "ingredients" needed to bring it into the world. We have already covered this ground. The millions of potential cardholders aligned with the *PARALLEL* ethos are already in place. They are waiting for the *PARALLEL* Economy but do not know it. The philanthropic-oriented money needed to create the *Climate Emergency Bank* is also ready and waiting for these ideas to make themselves visible. The *PARALLEL* Economy is both so far away from manifesting because it is just a figment of my imagination and so close because the readiness for it is screaming for a chance to be in this world and express itself.

Chapter 17: The Pitch – Climate Emergency Credit Card

<u>The Pitch</u>

If you have one iota of concern or interest about global warming, keep reading.

Apply for the *Climate Emergency Card ("E" Card)*. You use it like any other card with one major difference.

The *"E" Card* is backed by the not-for-profit *Climate Emergency Bank* which is dedicated solely to rewilding and decarbonizing and meeting the global warming crisis.

No other bank or credit card in the world is doing this.

Climate activism needs you. Our planetary life support systems need you.

No gimmicks. We play by a few simple rules.

<u>Rule #1</u>:

Your *Climate Emergency Card* will direct all the profits it earns to work with and support environmental organizations, climate scientists, activists, entrepreneurial climate-centric initiatives, educators and thought leaders, researchers, and allied media from around the globe.

<u>Rule #2</u>:

We mean business for the climate. Where and when necessary, your *"E" Card* will lead to create any needed initiatives to fulfill its rewilding and decarbonizing mission. We are not reckless, or cavalier about risk-taking. But we need to take them. The global warming clock is ticking.

<u>Rule #3</u>:

Your *Climate Emergency Card* is transparent in its operation. No secrets. We aim to win your understanding and trust.

<u>Rule #4</u>:

The *Climate Emergency Bank* is a charitable 501.c3 in its official not-for-profit mission, but it is not asking you for charity. Our *"E" Card* wants to win your business by giving you far-more of what you want than other cards do.

What do you "really" want?

Convention says you want rewards – cash back – airline miles etc. Agreed, we think you want rewards. Who doesn't? But we believe you want something bigger, something that has never been tested in a focus group.

- We think you want more sanity in this world. We think you want more justice.
- We think you want to do something about climate change and don't know what that is.
- We think you want to make a difference.
- We think you want to believe the *Climate Emergency Card* could be for real.
- We think you want to be part of the climate crisis solution...if there was a practical way.

And there is one – a way to integrate practicality, rewards, and a change the world mission.

Consider the *Climate Emergency* Card. It will give you.

An annual card charge of $0 to $infinity. Do what you can.

Interest rate charges on any outstanding debt at 33% less than traditional charge cards.

Standard fees for cash advances, balance transfers and late fees, also at 33% less.

Discounts at participating *PARALLEL* Card merchants whenever you use the *"E"* Card.

Pride to be a part of a global movement championing a response to the climate crisis.

But how?

How can our *Climate Emergency* Card offer you lower interest and fees than the big companies? Simple, we are not building stadiums with our name on it. We have no shareholders expecting profits. We are not paying million-dollar salaries to anyone. We will not be situated in lavish office buildings. We are not spending big bucks on advertising campaigns to win you over.

And in addition to the above reasons – we are compelled to find a way. Business-as-usual is unable to meet the climate crisis. We need a // reality to lead the way and prove that the impossible is not that.

PARALLEL Rewards

We will create a merchant's discount program better than your typical 2% or 3% cash back card offers. No other card can do this because, with few exceptions, no other card has a "reason-to-be" besides benefiting itself.

The *PARALLEL* economic vision will attract millions of businesses that are allied with our cause and want to attract customers such as yourself by offering a discount to you on all *"E" Card* purchases.

The Merchant's Program will take some time to build, but 5% - 10% discounts are possible.

Start with us. Stick with us. Help build the *PARALLEL* economic movement.

PARALLEL Pay

// Pay will be a Venmo-type alternative backed by the not-for-profit *Climate Emergency Bank*. It will allow you to purchase items, split checks, rent payments etc. without using a credit card.

Contactless transactions linked to your *Climate Emergency Card* are also possible. Like Venmo, *PARALLEL Pay* services will be free except for a 3% charge for *"E"* Credit Card transactions.

Don't forget Rule #1. All profits go towards re-wilding and decarbonizing.

Stay tuned to learn more about *PARALLEL Pay*.

Finally

Traditional forms of climate activism are critically needed, but they are also proving to be not enough. None have taken on the for-profit economy that simply cannot help itself from being about itself.

The Climate "E" *Card* is part of a growing parallel economic movement dedicated to fighting climate change that competes with but aims, as a goal, to creatively ally with its competition. Sounds like a contradiction. Yes, but this is the challenge of building the biggest "For-the-Climate" tent possible. Everyone is a potential ally.

A *PARALLEL* Economy is a grand idea. But big ideas are the only ones that can tackle the climate crisis.

What makes the *PARALLEL* Economy big is you – your buy-in and commitment to believing that you and hundreds of millions like you are ready to be united into a game-changing movement with a single purpose.

To create an alternative happy or happier ending to "The Global Warming Story."

Join the *PARALLEL* Movement – Make the *Climate Emergency Card* your everyday credit card.

Chapter 18: Fearless Imagining

There are many directions to explore in considering the *PARALLEL* economic paradigm. No doubt there are low hanging fruit choices that strategically make good business sense and will accelerate the // movement. However, I am not ready to introduce that degree of practical granularity here.

Right now, I am painting with broad brush strokes of possibility. To do so presents a double-edged sword. If I don't put more flesh on the bones, the *PARALLEL* Economy may come across to some as just a quixotic big idea, an abstraction – all talk, not enough action. But if I do or when I do, that "flesh" may seem preposterous, also quixotic and come across as "too much information."

I have decided that fearless imagining is needed. What follows is my attempt to make *the PARALLEL* Economy real and potent, in effect, to bring it alive and capable of being a force that helps express the urgency that Bill McKibben, Greta Thunberg, Naomi Klein and many others pine for.

PARALLEL-a-zon

One intriguing parallel road to venture down centers around Amazon®. This monolithic super-company is daunting to even approach. It is such a ubiquitous force in our collective sphere for better and for worse. What I am certain of is that Amazon cannot go untouched by //. There must be a parallel choice to challenge some of Amazon's ubiquity.

What could that possibly look like? What is our first move? Do we venture into the realm of cloud computing where Amazon has made massive investments and is burrowed deep, deep in our global digital infrastructure/architecture? Do we set our sights on developing a // to the Amazon owned Whole Foods Markets? Does the *PARALLEL* Economy make its mark in the consumer marketplace?

Is there any vulnerability to be found in this trillion-dollar empire that has been developing for the last 25 years? I am not sure. Since I am most familiar with the consumer marketplace, I am naturally pulled in that direction. But remember, I am not pouring cement.

Setting aside the Amazon vulnerabilities question, what I am clear on is that the *PARALLEL* Economy conception of Amazon does not mean becoming just an Amazon twin with a different focus – re-wilding and decarbonizing. Any singular obsession, whether it be noble quests like tackling global warming or profit-making to enrich shareholders can be misguided and the cause of damaging unintended consequences.

A //-a-zon that would ignore its impact on Main Street USA; that would squeeze municipalities dry to get tax advantages; that opportunistically cherry picks and destroys competitors with its own branding; that creates pace of work pressures on its employees that causes burn-out; all in service to its singular focus would miss the point of its coming into being.

Simply switching out profit-making for re-wilding and decarbonizing would not reflect the change in consciousness that the *PARALLEL* Economy must demand of itself and then emulate as a model.

As such, what I foresee is a network of independent businesses united in its sharing of ecological and social justice values and utilizing the *PARALLEL* Marketplace platform for the greatest climate activism impact possible. Challenging? Yes. Impossible? No.

A //-a-zon will compete successfully with Amazon wherever and however it decides to jump into the fray for several reasons.

Consumers will respond to the climate change mission by supporting the *PARALLEL* Marketplace.

Merchants will appreciate *PARALLEL's* non-compete policy on behalf of their success.

Everyone will like the win-win-win // Discount Program.

PARALLEL will deliver service, convenience, choices, and reliability in its own unique, game-changing way. People do not shop Amazon because they love enriching Jeff Bezos or its gorilla bullying tactics.

Of course, I am impatient to know more of the specifics and share them with you. But I am offering a sketch here and not a blueprint.

And this is a start. In my mind's eye, I am standing in front of a doorway that has a sign attached to it that says in big bold red letters "STOP – THERE IS NO DOORWAY HERE." I know this is a lie. I know the *PARALLEL* Economy lives behind it. And I think within that knowing lies something like //-a-zon.

McPARALLELS

I mentioned this idea earlier. And please, don't get thrown off by the name or any name I am throwing out. It is my way of injecting fun into the creative process. Otherwise, it is a dull existence.

Imagine a fast-food choice with a climate friendly focus that champions regenerative agriculture, carbon sequestration, fair trade purchasing, Amazon rainforest and Great Northern Forest protection and so on. It would be a melting pot of food, eating philosophies, local and regional agriculture production, cultural and ethnic diversity, climate activism, the arts, music and who knows what else?

And of course, a discount offered when using the *Climate Emergency Card.*

Simultaneously imagine a parallel to the institutional food distribution system dominated by the likes of US Foods, United Naturals, KEHE, and Sysco. Let's call it for ease *PARALLEL* FOOD SERVICE.

// FOOD SERVICE

PARALLEL FOOD SERVICE (// FS) would distribute to Mc//s and, of course, as far and wide as possible in the institutional food realm. There is a legitimate business opportunity here, which means an incredible opportunity for funding climate activism. All that is needed is a well-capitalized challenger like // FS who lives for very different reasons than these established behemoths do.

Obviously, these BIG ideas do not just magically appear, but it also does not take magic for them to do so. It takes the money, the ethos, the know-how, the leadership, the execution and perhaps most importantly the readiness in the world-at-large.

I am writing as confidently as I am because I believe the "readiness" is in place. // FOOD SERVICE is sitting in the ether waiting for its moment. The moment is defined by you and me, us, and millions more coming together as a movement that is tired of feeling disempowered; tired of waiting for political ineptness to stop; tired of the narrowness of corporate profit-making; and tired of waiting for financial institutions to grow a spine and take more risks because if not now than when.

Enough is enough.

In the ether also lies the *PARALLEL Climate Action Food E'mporium*, the retail and pioneering *PARALLEL* CAFÉ.

THE PARALLEL CAFÉ

First, this could be tricky territory because the aim of the *PARALLEL* CAFÉ initiative is not to hurt food cooperatives and smaller stores. And // FOOD SERVICE wants to become their go-to wholesale foods distributor. So, creating a retail *PARALLEL* supermarket-type outlet might be problematic if it were a competitor. But there is a way.

That way is the careful targeting of the location of // CAFÉ outlets such that they compete with mainstream supermarket chains and Whole Foods stores but not smaller community co-ops or mom & pop outlets.

Second to note is consideration of the word "compete." Again, the point of the *PARALLEL* Economy paradigm I am trying to bring to light is not to create a parallel twin that looks much like a Safeway, Publix, or Whole Foods. This would be failure.

In addition to its re-wilding and decarbonizing raison d'etre, the CAFÉ is imagined as an innovative retail foods concept built around reducing the need for packaging and plastics and introducing the next generation of bulk foods dispensing, convenience, and resulting advantageous consumer pricing.

The CAFÉ will also re-introduce the idea of community volunteer labor (in exchange for a food discount), a foundation of the early food cooperative impulse. There are good reasons why the implementation of this impulse fell out of favor and good reasons to problem solve around those reasons and build a win-win economic model for volunteers and the CAFÉ operation.

And there is more. The *PARALLEL* CAFÉ concept will revolutionize onsite glass and stainless container washing, sanitizing and re-use. This will require a change in behaviors and expectations from consumers and as such will cater at the outset to early adapters. Not everyone will be ready for new ways to purchase food, but this pioneering is necessary. In a deliberate iterative process, the CAFÉ will change the face of retail food purchasing and reduce the size and impact of its environmental footprint...forever.

Remember, 5 steps forward and 2 back will change our world. The question we need to keep asking ourselves is.... How do we do that?

<u>Two Dynamic Food Concepts – *The Café Eatery* and *The Ice Cream Universe*</u>

To bring to the *PARALLEL* CAFÉ a much bigger audience than just the early adapter cohorts, two dynamic food concept magnets are envisioned. One is an actual café I am calling the *Café Eatery* with a revolutionary seating system designed for (thanks to post-Covid lessons) air circulation/purification, comfort, social distancing and just plain old privacy.

The *Eatery* will feature street foods from around the world, an Artisan empanada universe, global traditional baked goods, and classic ethnic desserts. And, of course, a universe of teas, coffees, fresh juices, shakes etc.

Speaking of universe, the second food concept magnet that will be housed inside the CAFÉ is the *Ice Cream Universe.*

The *Ice Cream Universe* brings together traditional and not so traditional frozen desserts from around the world. From no churn Indian Cardamon Kulfi to Italian Gelato to Japanese Mochi to Iranian Faloodeh to Turkish Dondurma to Israeli Halva Ice Cream.... You get the idea. There is a universe of possibilities, dairy and non-dairy, on sticks, in cones of every kind, cups, sandwiches and who knows what else once this gets going. And all made in small-batches right in the *PARALLEL* CAFÉ's ice cream central mini-factory.

To point out the obvious, the theme lying within these two food magnet ideas is the globe and inclusiveness. And this is what *PARALLEL* Economy is all about – a globe in crisis needs a globe in action. Also, to move beyond moments of action and build a movement, inclusiveness in every way possible needs to be cultivated.

There are so many reasons for "separation" between us to prevail. Nationality, race, religion, ethnicity, social class, economic status, sexual orientation, political affiliations, right-to-choose and gun control have all taken center stage to do the job. And sadly, sometimes separation may be unavoidable.

Many scoff at the very idea of human-caused climate change. I profoundly disagree with them and will oppose them in every peaceful way possible. But I will not demonize them. Some of these people will love the *Ice Cream Universe* or the *Café Eatery* setting and its Stuffed Peruvian Empanadas or the Gata zesty Armenian pastries. The point is a *PARALLEL* economic reality welcomes everyone regardless of their alignment and engagement with the global warming crisis.

Chapter 19: You get the idea

Banking, credit cards, online shopping, wholesale food distribution, restaurants, retail food sales and related complementary concepts are just the beginning of building a *PARALLEL* Economy.

// Media lives somewhere in the queue. Possibly // Travel? // Insurance? A *PARALLEL* version of Airbnb? Climate TV?

You get the idea. The challenge along the way is to remember that the *PARALLEL* Economy is not about the *PARALLEL* Economy. It does not exist for itself so it can look in the mirror and say, "Look at it me! I am big. I am powerful." No.

Rather, *PARALLEL* is about empowering and uniting and building a movement that shifts the way we grow, consume, travel, build, landscape, heat, power, recycle and restore. Its focus is near term and long term. Everything with a carbon footprint is a target of consideration.

Every ecosystem, whether it be grasslands, mangroves, marshes, oceans, forestland etc. that has been undone, is undermined, or under threat is a focus of the Climate Activist Movement (CAM) and global plan of action.

Remember, the Climate Activist Movement (CAM) represents the web of life mapped across the globe and framed as crisis areas needing re-wilding. The priorities within each key area are identified and the action plans down to the last detail are specified to assure maximum results. The Climate Activist Agreement and related Movement is the brains behind the brute cash *PARALLEL* Economy brawn.

Without this in-depth continuity and understanding, you have a piecemeal quilt...a little of this, a little of that. You have silos and competition for scarce resources. The big picture stays illusive and the obstacles to establish a united and coordinated Climate Activist Movement stay formidable.

All of these *PARALLEL* Economy imaginings are more than just a tantrum of ideas. They are remedies of consequence. I have been weaving a fabric of vertically integrated solutions starting with a foundational funding philosophy and strategy. Dependent on that philosophy is a wealth of entrepreneurial initiatives all with their own *PARALLEL* twist.

<u>These are not normal times</u>.

The point of it all is to consume more smartly; to usurp power from those who cannot see beyond their own self-interest and to re-orient their priorities and related decision-making despite themselves; to become a global political force; to materialize a transformative scale of brute cash; and to be an organizing beacon (CAM) to direct that cash on behalf of achieving the greatest re-wilding and de-carbonizing impact possible. In short – A Revolution in Activism.

If we look at this *PARALLEL* conception in the normal way with our regular thinking caps on, it is too big, way too big. But these are not normal times. We are not facing a normal situation.

In fact, we need a mobilization with an urgency behind it like never before. I am trying to capture both the letter and the spirit of a way to meet that urgency. I have called it the *Climate Emergency Plan.*

<u>Reality Check</u>

Global warming is accelerating. The usual suspects are to blame – a powerful fossil fuels industry, wasteful consumerism, planned obsolescence, and a myriad other shortcomings attributed to our 21st century living.

Something else stands out. Climate activism impact appears to have hit a wall. Although public awareness and angst about global warming has grown dramatically, activist leaders like Bill McKibben, Naomi Klein and Greta Thunberg all bemoan the fact that our planetary life support systems are more imperiled than ever. The sum of the prolific actions of environmental organizations; the inspiring worldwide climate strikes; the attention-grabbing youth-for-climate rallies; high profile lawsuits; and the many celebrity activists are all proving to be not enough. We are faltering.

How does the activist community navigate around or through this obstructive wall? How do we make haste to change the narrative from our faltering to altering the advance of climate change?

The change needed is two-fold.

First, climate activism needs to become central in transforming our economic system to reflect its sustainable values and goals. To do so means to stop deferring to the "old guard" that dominates the global flow of money and to create a parallel "new guard" that serves as an independent force offering new choices and representing more enlightened social values, financial influence, and economic leadership.

Second, we must energize the vast amount of resigned, cynical, and uninformed human potential (including its capital and buying power) haplessly sitting on the sidelines of everyday living and unite it, empower it, and put it to work for the climate. When meaning and purpose are shared by millions, anything and everything is possible.

Our faltering will begin to end when we find our way to manifesting these two understandings.

Think of the *Climate Emergency Plan* in its entirety as a vaccine to prevent unbridled entropy – the natural tendency to disorder and separation; the tendency for our human energy to disperse, fizzle and lose its organization and cohesiveness.

It aims to counter this dissolution or to at least moderate it and to bring people together, but not just in moments of inspiring and uplifting actions and not just within their silos of activism. Rather, the plan's two-part ambition, the *PARALLEL* Economy and the Climate Activist Movement (CAM), is to bring people together as both a movement without boundaries and one that requires little effort or sacrifice to join or participate in.

The difference between a moment and a movement is the difference between a tree and a forest of trees. Presently, there are a lot of moments of activism, a lot of trees – conferences, strikes, lawsuits, books, environmental organizations, and much more. The fight against global warming and the failure of our planetary life support systems certainly needs these moments, these trees, but only if they become tied together into a forest ecosystem or movement to become the systemic change that is needed.

Biologists, ecologists, oceanographers, environmentalists and many from other scientific disciplines have devoted themselves to the understanding of our biosphere's natural systems and what makes them viable, resilient, and integral to carbon capture and global climate stability. We have invested a lot in knowing how our natural ecosystems tick.

Where we are lacking and where we need to apply a similar scale of investment and determination is to the understanding of our human systems, nature, dynamics, and behaviors.

What would make our organization, as a species, capable of meeting a nemesis of its own making – global warming?

Without this complementary understanding of our human selves, the movement that we need is struggling to be born.

The *Climate Emergency Plan's* ambition is to facilitate this birth. It is evolutionary in its aim to withstand the aforementioned natural tendency to disorder (entropy) that is often the undoing of effective and sustained organizational initiatives. It is revolutionary in its aim to create something that is globally cohesive and capable of IMPACT on a planetary scale.

But to be clear, this *Emergency Plan* does not require personal enlightenment nor economic and political revolution. It does not require a radical shift in the consciousness of humanity. That is because those who acknowledge this crisis and engage to meet it will re-direct what is to what must be – not perfectly, but good enough to cause a shift and make a difference.

What is today is capitalism serving as a means for economic survival but at the expense of our planetary life support systems. What must be tomorrow is also a means for economic survival but without that self-destructive price tag. The *Climate Emergency Plan* will give people around the globe a viable way to be empowered by their purchasing power, a path, in effect, to dictate the future behavior of not only corporations but of any representative democracy, also dependent upon the will of the people.

The point being, people do not just buy, they also vote. Corporate profit-making will not be banished but it will have to compete with a *PARALLEL* economic reality determined to educate consumers and offer them as many *PARALLEL* branded choices and *PARALLEL* aligned choices as possible.

These new climate-friendly choices and our receptive response to them will bend and re-order our societal values and in turn the behaviors that are driving us down this global warming road.

PART 6

More Reality

Chapter 20: The Titanic of Surfside, Florida

<u>Do You See the Parallel?</u>

The third-deadliest non-deliberate structural engineering failure in United States history occurred on June 24, 2021. A 12-story condominium high rise collapsed in Surfside, Florida. 98 people died affecting families from around the world including Argentina, Colombia, and Paraguay.

During the investigation, a 2018 engineering report of the structure surfaced pointing to *"abundant cracking and spalling"* of concrete columns, beams and walls in the parking garage. The same firm detailed in an earlier report that the ground floor pool deck of the building was resting on a concrete slab that *"had major structural damage."*

At the time of the collapse, the condo association had approved an assessment of $15 million for repairs — a process they began more than two years after receiving a report of major structural damage in the building.

Perhaps some of the Surfside residents knew of this report or even read it. Many, no doubt, saw the cracking and deterioration of the concrete in the parking garage, maybe even on a daily basis. The pool area problems were also probably obvious. The threatening news of the significant cost of the repairs probably spread through the condominium complex like wildfire, even if the details did not. And the engineering science was not controversial. The damage was real.

Do you see the parallel to our climate change situation?

The building in the minds of those living in it and/or responsible for it was too big to fail. It was their "world" and it felt big. You could count on it. It had stood for 40 years. How could it just, in an instant, pancake into a heap of rubble and lost lives?

And yet those same minds were also surrounded by information and empirical evidence that arguably should have galvanized immediate action. The foundation their lives were built on was literally crumbling. They were warned, not of the imminent collapse, but of major structural damage.

There was evidence plain to see. Yet, everything still "felt" normal enough. The elevators worked. The building was not a leaning tower. People were not scared to death. The dots that were obvious (crumbling concrete pillars) did not connect to the dots that were not. And a reality too big to fail, just as the RMS Titanic was too big to sink, collapsed into nothingness.

Most of us are not paying attention.

Climate scientists have been sounding the global warming alarm for decades now. Our planetary life support systems are a reality far more complex and invisible than the failing concrete support pillars of that 12-story building. Earth failure is not only inconceivable, but also incomprehensible because we don't see ocean currents, much less understand them. We don't see CO_2.

Most of us do not attribute the shrinking reservoirs of Lake Mead (in California and Nevada) that supplies water to 20 million people and Lake Powell (located in Arizona and Utah) that supplies water to 40 million people out West to the shaky "12-story building" under attack in South America called the Amazon Rain Forest.

This April 2024, the average global level of atmospheric CO_2 rose to 419.3 parts per million (ppm), a record high. The last time CO_2 levels were so elevated was 3 million years ago when sea levels were 100 feet higher and we, so called modern humans, did not exist.

There have been hundreds of heat related deaths in Maricopa County, Arizona this July 2024, which includes Phoenix at 118F. At least 1300 people died at this year's haj, an Islamic pilgrimage in Saudi Arabia as temperatures reached 120F.

In fact, there has been a sudden rise in daily global average temperatures attributed to above average temperatures in Antarctica. Sea ice levels have lowered, which in turn is heating up the Southern Ocean.

Most of us are not paying attention. We may be inconvenienced and decide to buy an air conditioner. That's about it. Many of us care, but don't know what to do. Some are more engaged within a wide spectrum of activism. But so far, our lives and lifestyles are going on and will go on, just as the lives in that Surfside condo did until the unimaginable happened.

The condo association received its alarming engineering report. We, citizens of the planet, have been receiving dire reports and alarming global warming trends for decades. The condo residents saw the deterioration of their building, just as we see or learn of unprecedented sea-level rise, decimated coral reefs, rising global temperatures, and disappearing glaciers.

The condominium residents had to face the cost of repair and did not in a timely way, just as we collectively are confronted with the costs of our fossil fuel addiction and the loss of mangroves and peat bogs and their natural carbon sequestering capabilities. Yet, we are also not responding in a timely way with the necessary actions and adaptations.

You see where this is headed. Hence, my dedication at the beginning of this book.

To the many millions who will be displaced, the many who will die, suffer, and live lives without the stability and security of the Earths planetary life support systems.

To the species that will become extinct because of climate change.

And to all the future prayers, tears, and trauma needlessly spoken, shed, and felt because we humans chose to react to tragedy rather than act to prevent it.

And prayers, tears, trauma, blame, and lawsuits are exactly what followed after the Surfside tragedy.

The *Climate Emergency Plan* is presented as a path to prevent the predictable and the inevitable losses that are coming. Why not unite in solidarity in front of the "building" collapse rather than unite afterwards in shared grief and bewilderment?

Chapter 21: I was not able to walk my talk.

I tried to bring some of my *PARALLEL* Economy ideas to the real world in all-out effort from April 2019 through June 2020. You may note that the Covid-19 pandemic dropped into our lives within this timeframe.

I did not succeed.

Here is a synopsis and what I learned.

My journey started with an outreach to climate activist and author Bill McKibben. I had just read the Guardian newspaper April 2019 open letter that I mentioned back in Chapter 1. Bill had signed it along with Greta Thunberg, Naomi Klein and 20 other prominent climate activists.

I found Bill's email address and astoundingly he responded to me in one day. I was impressed and grateful.

Bill and I had a few inconsequential exchanges until February 18, 2020. I had introduced the *Climate Emergency Credit Card* idea to him in a 3-pager attachment on February 5 (See Addendum). On the 18th he wrote *"This strikes me as a fascinating idea. Thanks for good thinking."*

The net of Bill's engagement was a key introduction to an executive at the Amalgamated Bank, the largest B Corp bank in the United States. This seemed like a major breakthrough. As it unfolded, there was enough interest at Amalgamated to lead to a further introduction, but not the engagement I was hoping for.

This is the nature of entrepreneuring or questing. You try and try....and keep trying ad infinitum.

My brother Arnie (who had joined me on this ride) and I took heart that this next spark of possibility introduced us to one of the largest philanthropic organizations in the United States: *The William and Flora Hewlett Foundation*.

Simultaneously, Arnie and I found another promising lead with an executive at the San Francisco based *RSF Social Finance*. We learned that RSF had made over $500 million in loans, grants, and investments supporting social enterprises in the areas of food, agriculture, education, the arts, and ecological stewardship. Again, our 3-pager *Climate Emergency Credit Card* introduction cracked the door to the following response and very encouraging prospect.

"What an honor to receive this thoughtful proposal. Thank you. I am in complete agreement with your diagnosis and analysis and am very interested in the initiative you suggest. The financial system, by extension the banking system and our concept of money is built on extraction and self-centeredness. If we want to support healing the planet and communities, we can't do that with a broken financial system.....I'm excited to explore this idea."

I learned an invaluable lesson because our simpatico outlooks should have led to an encouraging outcome and next steps. And it did not. I lacked the flexibility to move us forward together. Some of my historic entrepreneurial scars were skewing my expectations of this executive. I wanted his enthusiasm and alignment with our ideas to translate into a degree of financial risk-taking and commitment on behalf of the *Climate Emergency Card* initiative that he could not make.

I was too identified with my point of view and related expectations. They clouded the way I needed to respond to the challenges as the entrepreneur/catalyzer. I did not discern well what was a fixed, immoveable object for an established financial entity with fiduciary responsibilities like RSF Social Finance and what was actually moveable and hence workable for this executive.

I drew red lines where, in hindsight, I should not have.

The *Hewlett Foundation* contact directed us to the *New Energy Nexus*, an international non-profit funded by Hewlett that supports clean energy entrepreneurs with funds, accelerators and networks. The Climate Fintech lead there at the time responded below to our trusty credit card 3-pager.

"We are keenly interested in your Climate Emergency Credit Card concept, and its journey looking forward. It would be wonderful to discuss this project and ways to work together in greater detail."

Here there was another "no result" despite again the keen interest. There is something instructive to take from this experience.

It is not a given that you start out being sophisticated and savvy when venturing out on a new limb, even if you have already been on countless others.

The *New Energy Nexus* folks were sizing up our *Climate Emergency Credit Card* initiative as a business start-up. Arnie and I were not. We didn't have a business plan. We had no LLC, no financing, and no management team to speak of besides ourselves. Viewed through the traditional lens of a start-up, we were wholly lacking. And Arnie and I wholly knew that.

The disconnect was that Arnie and I were trying to introduce a visionary paradigm (though we hadn't named it the *PARALLEL* Economy yet) using the *Climate Emergency Credit Card* idea as an anchor. We were not trying to entice *the New Energy Nexus* and Hewlett to invest in our start-up. Rather we hoped they would invest, utilizing their universe of resources and expertise, in fleshing out and manifesting the *Emergency Card* idea.

Contrary to what most entrepreneurs want, Arnie and I had no interest in personal ownership, upsides, or jobs in our perceived "start-up." As such, we were odd ducks.

We couldn't change how the *New Energy Nexus* perceived us, and we could not bend to their will and make ourselves into the start-up we did not want to be. We were too early stage. The feasibility study our *Emergency Credit Card* aspiration needed and which we could not finance ourselves fell outside of their business-as-usual approach.

We found ourselves in a mutually acknowledged impasse.

Arnie and I were in the right place or certainly right enough with both the *New Energy Nexus* and *RSF Social Finance,* but we weren't ready with the tools to thread the needle.

We tried mightily, but effort does not ensure success.

The silver lining of course is what we learned.

Also, within this timeframe the Covid pandemic was raging. Everything was shut down. There was a palpable and pervasive fear in everyday living. Maybe that was a factor in our mindset and outlook.

Chapter 22: Sorry Kids

Taking into account the "non-results" above does not negate the fact that one of the most prominent climate activists in the world, Bill McKibben, thought our *Climate Emergency Credit Card* was a *"fascinating idea."* It does not negate the fact that the Amalgamated Bank officer in charge of entertaining new ideas thought enough of our initiative to introduce us to the Hewlett Foundation with assets of $14 billion at the time. Then a decision-maker at Hewlett sufficiently engaged with our ideas to direct us to the *New Energy Nexus.* Those folks were also intrigued. And then there was RSF Social Finance and one of its executives' certain alliance with our thinking and ideas.

Despite this impressive across-the-board engagement, Arnie and I struck out.

Yes, our resumes were lacking in banking expertise and insider pedigree. Yes, we were very early stage without a business plan, start-up funding, or LLC. But, on the other hand, are potentially paradigm shifting ideas a dime a dozen?

By convention and in ordinary times, the failed outcomes Arnie and I experienced make sense, paradigm shifting or not. But are these ordinary times? Are our planetary life support systems really threatened or not? Is the approach of climate change catastrophe hyperbolic fear mongering or not? Is climate change activism and our human response to global warming faltering or not?

If threatened planetary life support systems, climate change catastrophe, and our human faltering are all simultaneously in motion then certainly decision-making "by convention" lacks the immediacy that is required; then certainly ordinary times are in the rear-view mirror; and the outcome, our *Climate Emergency Card* inspiration sputtering into oblivion, makes no sense.

But this is the time we are in. The "No Sense Era." The time when the most biologically rich savanna in the world and a huge carbon sink, the Brazilian

Cerrado (3X times the size of Texas), is being razed to produce soy, beef, cotton, and sugar cane; the time when United States lawmakers can find $1.7 trillion dollars to invest in the problematic F-35 fighter jet but procrastinate about funding high-speed rail.

Regarding high-speed rail, Amtrak estimates that the cost to replace its existing Northeast Corridor (457 miles) with true high-speed rail would be $500 million per mile. At first glance, this stated amount must be a typo. The cost is obscene. But let's put this high-speed rail cost per mile (which isn't a typo) into the context of the F-35 debacle. A quick calculation shows that $1.7 trillion dollars buys 3400 miles of high-speed rail or more than seven Northeast Corridors installations.

What are we doing? This is our $1.7 trillion enriching Lockheed Martin; our sacrifice; our ambivalence; and our disempowerment. How do we explain this failing to our children and our grandchildren when their planetary life support systems falter?

<u>Kids, it's simple</u>.

The explanation goes like this.

Kids, it's simple. Climate change does not present itself as an imminent threat despite all of the handwringing on the subject. It doesn't matter enough that we adults are educated and know differently. Amazon Rain Forest this, ocean acidification that, CO2 this and peat bogs and mangroves that, and on and on. All the dire related facts in the world are not yet internalized such that collectively they evoke the shame and horror of leaving you an overheated future world that will likely impose extreme weather, make many parts of the globe unlivable, accelerate the dying off of key ecosystems like coral reefs, wetlands, alpine areas and the Arctic and displace and kill millions of you without recourse.

Our lukewarm response to global warming is screaming in its inadequacy. The obvious disconnect from an impending disastrous reality persists. The failure to viscerally feel the gun pointed at the temple of future generations is why there are a million reasons or excuses for things to either stay the same or change, but only modestly and within the confines allowed by convention and the ponderous, rudderless thinking that accompanies it.

In contrast, when a crisis and a threat really become personal to the bone, the brain recalibrates, and synapses start reshuffling themselves. Our amygdala's take over. In that moment you and me (we) know what we have to do, and hells bells, we do everything in our power and beyond to do it.

Hells bells maybe ringing, but collectively, we are not hearing them. And "political leadership" has all but disappeared offering us very little guidance to heed. The words "political" and "leadership" have become like two north poles of a magnet. They repel each other. The political or tribalism half seems to be innate for us human beings. It cannot escape the gravity of its own self-serving nature. The leadership part lies latent, enslaved by ideology and/or the fear of making a mistake and the subsequent political costs.

Of course, there is other "leadership" found within public activism, environmental organizations, not-for-profit initiatives, and entrepreneurial endeavors, but no matter how impressive, determined, earnest and accomplished this is, its effect is muted and has not elicited *"the necessary urgency needed to prevent our planetary life support systems from spiraling into collapse."*

Our amygdalae are at rest and getting pudgy. Global warming, so far, remains a crisis in name only. Sorry kids.

You see the parallel?

Tasting real can be humbling and disturbing. Today, I had a particularly discouraging and sobering thought.

What is discouraging is unrelated to climate change or, at first glance, is seemingly so. It is my remembering of the 2012 Sandy Hook Elementary shooting in Newtown, Connecticut and the 2018 shooting at Marjory Stoneman Douglas High School in Parkland, Florida.

But it is related.

How much more precious than the slaughter of our children does it have to get to ban semi-automatic weapons or at least reasonably restrict their access? How many mothers and fathers, grandparents, aunts and uncles and countless others have been ripped apart by this senseless carnage?

And in turn how many gun control activists, many of whom are the loved ones of victims, remain in shock and disbelief that despite their loss, outrage, and advocacy, despite the fact that 56% -70% of Americans support them and a related ban, semi-automatic weapons persist, and the killing goes on and on?

How much more precious than the upending of our planetary life support systems does it have to get before there is a full-scale mobilization to stop or slow down CO2 build-up and global warming? How many coral reefs do we have to lose? How many tens of thousands of acres of the Amazon must be burned year after year? Why have large corporations prevailed and government policies failed even though a majority of Americans believe in human fueled climate change? And not just Americans. The majority of people around the globe (surveyed by Pew Research Center in 2018) from Brazil to South Korea to Kenya recognize our warming globe as a major threat.

And logically, why would I ever think that if the slaughter of our children doesn't move us to instant action on an assault weapon ban that something more abstract and complex to understand like the acidification of our oceans would result in the actions and changes needed, like shutting down CO2 emissions on scale, to make a difference?

You see the parallel?

Pick Your Crazy

Of course, what I am alluding to here is the obvious impossible chasm to span that practical people point to when they sympathetically scoff or roll their eyes at the notion of a unifying movement or a *PARALLEL* economy. *McPARALLELS*, ridiculous. *//-a-zon*, absurd!! *The Climate Emergency Credit Card,* good luck!!!

I get it. I can't tell the scoffers and eye rollers, *"You're wrong."* But they also cannot tell me what they are right about unless it's clima-geddon.

Pick your crazy.

The crazy of resignation and hopelessness, that is, the crazy of the status quo that has us all on the Titanic where on some decks the music plays on; where some dutifully, if not passionately, scurry around chaotically trying to plug the leaks; where some people are ushered onto life rafts; and where others are inundated by terror and diminishment, if not displacement and death.

Or the crazy of hopefulness where our human potential is not ignored but rather embraced in its possibility to manifest something that is needed; in the crazy that has us mobilizing together because we are perilously together on a warming planet, our children and future generations in tow.

Chapter 23: A report from the future?

"Record dry conditions in South America have led to wildfires, power cuts and water rationing.

The world's largest river system, the Amazon, which sustains some 30 million people across eight countries is drying up.

In Brazil, wildfires fueled by searing heat and prolonged dry conditions have consumed vast swaths of forest, wetlands and pastures, with smoke spreading to 80 percent of the country. It has led to canceled classes, hospitalizations and a black dust coating the inside of homes.

To the south, in Paraguay, the Paraguay River has hit new lows. Ships are stranded and fishermen say their most valuable quarry — including the enormous surubí catfish — have all but disappeared, forcing many people to look for work elsewhere to feed their families.

The drought covers large parts of the Amazon rainforest, especially worrying because it is the globe's most important carbon sink, absorbing heat trapping gases. Dryer conditions diminish the forest's ability to take in those gases, worsening global warming.........

The drought is fueled by two trends linked to climate change, said Carlos Nobre, a Brazilian Scientist. First, a particularly strong El Niño weather pattern parched the region. While El Niños, a natural climate occurrence linked to warmer conditions in the tropical Pacific Ocean have caused droughts for millions of years, stronger El Niños have become more frequent as the planet warms. Second, the temperature in the North Atlantic has hit a new high, contributing to the drier conditions.

In the Amazon, the drought has crossed several unsettling milestones: never has so little rain fallen in the rainforest, never have dry conditions lasted so long, and never has such a vast region of the jungle been in drought."

No, it is now!

New York Times - Published Oct. 19, 2024. Updated Oct. 21, 2024 By Julie Turkewitz, Ana Ionova, and José María León Cabrera

Chapter 24: Bubbles

When I reflect back on "I was not able to walk my talk" one of the things that stands out and stands in the way are "bubbles".

Climate activism, celebrity, academia, politics, media and most human endeavors are subject to the propensity for insulating "bubbles" or cliques to form. It is natural. Bill McKibben probably has Greta Thunberg on speed dial. Actress Jane Fonda has directed her activist passion to climate change. No doubt, she is in the bubble with Bill and Greta and author Naomi Klein, actor Leonardo DiCaprio, climate change economist William Nordhaus and many more.

To be clear, I am not disparaging anyone who, through sustained diligence, sacrifice, and expertise, has become known, admired, influential, and accomplished.

What I am saying is that this propensity towards insider bubbles shrinks the gene pool of ideas. Dynamism suffers. Potential breakthroughs fail to see the light of day. It is difficult to penetrate the protective shield that bubbles surround themselves with. It's a problem.

Of course, I also realize it's a dilemma for prominent people to manage the myriad of queries that no doubt comes their way. They have to set limits and protect their privacy and personal space.

Sadly, bubbles slow the cross pollination of ideas and potential. If this is true or perceived to have some validity by those living in a bubble then the question, "What can be done?" deserves attention. Otherwise, the *impossible that will not fail us* may languish in obscurity because no one recognized who was knocking on the bubble door.

My suggestion is to have bubbles identify themselves as such and invite, once a year, for example, an open brainstorm or forum for creative ideas on any given subject. This would help to engage and build out the creative talent with who knows what potential and impact. Perhaps none. Perhaps something energizing, grand, and needed.

Why not do this?

Chapter 25: This is the time.

The messaging throughout this *Climate Emergency Plan* is all about the possible impossible. The climate problems we face are big and we, as individuals, are small. Naturally, we all get pushed into the SO-SO – the same old – same old – corner that whispers sweet nothings into our ears like "you are nothing, nothing." And also insists that there is no real "we" because how could there be? The notion is preposterous. After all, Donald Trump is President. We are so divided.

It is reasonable if not rational to think defeatedly.

But are we defeated? Do we have any agency in our lives to make a difference or must we stick our heads in the sand and stay ignorant or otherwise be doomed to resignation and powerlessness?

The possibility of agency and impact requires a leap of faith or a momentary suspension of disbelief. It is far easier to think or say "No" to the ideas in these pages than it is to say "Yes" or possibly "Yes."

This is the time for that leap and suspension of thinking-as-usual. Right now, we are not fulfilling our collective human potential as shapers and transformers of the future.

The *PARALLEL* Economy and Climate Activist Movement (CAM) are possible. We clearly have a cause to unite for. Now what?

My answer is to create our *PARALLEL* lives as a movement to manifest a Revolution in Activism.

We are cosmic.

Stepping back, I feel in awe of what unites us and connects us to this miraculous blue marble we all are living on.

Too many have forgotten or have not stayed connected to the fact that we are each truly part of this miracle, this impossible We are cosmic. Our bones, our hemoglobin have their origins in star dust. We are starry miracles for sure. Sounds impossible, doesn't it? It is time to make friends with the impossible.

I don't know if we are the only miraculous life in the universe, but we are all inarguably Earthlings.

To all Earthlings I say this. Life on planet Earth, the life that sustains us, the life that many enjoy is endangered by inalterably changing. We have all got a taste from our past Covid lives of what it means for life as we know it to dramatically change. Imagine if there had been no vaccines to bail us out; to return us to some approximation of normal. Imagine the ongoing disruption and the needed adaptations. What would the new normal have looked like?

Now, the second Trump presidency has descended upon us, the chaos of which is just getting started. What will bail us out in the face of his climate change denial and his "Drill Baby Drill" solution to all? Probably not a vaccine. This time the new normal will depend on us.

Stupid is as Stupid Does.

I understand that if this *Climate Emergency Plan* ever sees the light of day it will be politicized and demonized. Many will jump all over my suggestion to increase taxes on fossil fuels evoking a socialist take-over and engendering fear and resistance.

There will be Eeyore's, naysayers, and conspiracy theorists. Anything and everything will insist on obstructing. The SO-SO is a mighty force. It will fight for its life, but rest assured it will be ambivalent to yours and mine.

As the iconic Forest Gump said, "Stupid is as Stupid does." There are no mulligans or do-overs in this climate change story. Hurricane Helene, a once in a thousand-year devastating event, generated by record breaking water temperatures (near 90F) in the Gulf of Mexico, cannot be undone. The Amazon River is drying up and attributed to climate change and deforestation.

The cautionary tale of the frog lulled into complacency as the water surrounding him gets warmer and warmer and then hotter and hotter to his end is, of course, just for stupid frogs, certainly not us. Right?

Wrong. This is literally our story right now and to our end.

The only consolation I can offer is my belief that in the battle for hearts and minds there are far more people getting on board to accept the realities of climate change and the need to somehow respond to the crisis.

Point in fact, First Street (firststreet.org), a not-for-profit founded to "make the connection between climate change and financial risk at scale for financial institutions, companies, and governments" recently launched a suite of climate risk data for every for-sale property on Zillow. More than 80% of buyers now consider climate risk when purchasing a home.

Point in fact, properties impacted by FEMA's rapid rate increase have lost up to 54.1% in home value. This will certainly get the attention of many hearts and minds.

But also point in fact, responding to the crisis in an effectual way has not yet happened. Climate change activism, interventions, and policy making have not disrupted the arc of global warming.

Five years have passed since my awakening to the understanding that we are faltering, much of it in our Covid times and much of it living into my imagination – reality be damned.

Choosing to deliver on "the impossible that will not fail us" falls outside of anything and everything that is usual, predictable, expected and accepted. If I were writing the "Idiots Guide to Saving the World" or the "5 Easy Steps to Your *PARALLEL* Life," I would have already figured everything out to your and my amazement. But alas skepticism and doubt precede amazement. My hope is that this *Climate Emergency Plan* begins a conversation that will lead to such utilitarian book titles and our shared amazement and renewed hopefulness.

Afterwards

The most daunting aspect of effectively meeting the impossible is successfully competing for attention. We are inundated with information, stimuli, and distractions that have us clicking, watching, listening, and paying the most attention to those platforms and personalities who are best at grabbing our attention.

In this regard, it is not the cream (necessarily) that rises to the top, but arguably too often the clever, the crass, the well-connected, the monied, the shameless, and yes, the worthy as well.

Compounding this propensity towards mediocrity are the "bubbles" that I wrote about in Chapter 24 that have the tendency to cause individuals of influence, accomplishment, and/or celebrity to, in effect, "circle the wagons" to insure familiarity, continuity, control, and the leveraging of their influence.

The net is invisibility to those who do not have a knack for virality or the right knock for any given bubble door to open with some welcoming and inclusive cheer.

In order for the "impossible that will not fail us" to show up in our lives, its visibility cannot be impossible.

Everything that I have posited above in this *Climate Emergency Plan* conception – a dedicated not-for-profit or cooperative bank, the *Climate Emergency Credit Card*, the Climate Activist Movement (CAM) and the *PARALLEL* Economy enlivened by ideas like *//-a-zon* and McPARALLELs – is possible.

Banks exist, even B-Corp ones with climate-centric missions. Global accords are nothing new. The 2016 Paris Climate Agreement stands out. The Montreal Protocol, nailed down in 1987, is a global agreement to protect the ozone layer. There are multiple agreements, including regional and international ones, that have introduced controls to mitigate acid rain.

Mission driven and charitable entrepreneurial business initiatives are not a delusional ideal. Capitalism allows it. Newman's Own, founded in 1982 by the late actor Paul Newman, continues to use all of the money it receives from the sale of Newman's Own products to support children, their families, and their communities. The Newman slogan? "Let's Give It All Away." More than $600 million has been donated.

What caused the end of apartheid in South Africa? Global activism, charismatic leadership from within, and sustained international economic pressure including the large-scale divestment of assets held in endowments that were doing business in South Africa. It was a sustained aspirational movement. It happened.

It is a choice for everything to stay as it is.

As I reflect upon my journey so far, it is the *Climate Emergency Credit Card* that garnered the most attention and support. This was my initial inspiration and the starting point for crystallizing both the peoples' movement envisioned in the preceding pages and the economic engine to support and grow that movement.

The *Climate Emergency Card* opens the door for building out a *PARALLEL* Economic reality that collectively expresses the love for our Earth and the commitment to future generations. The *Card* helps to manifest something that most, if not all humans long for, that is purpose and belonging; that is to be a part of something bigger than ourselves.

I am not sure how many people think about their legacy, what they leave behind and what will endure when they pass on. I imagine for many, legacy means children and grandchildren. For some, it means a business and its influence and contributions that will carry on. Some people are able to create endowments or finance a wing of a hospital or a college auditorium with their name attached to it.

Generations also leave legacies and identities. The "Greatest Generation," people born between 1901 and 1927, came of age during what became known as the "American Century" of technological and economic growth.

Air conditioning, courtesy of Mr. Carrier. Manned flight thanks to the pioneering of the Wright brothers. Tea bags, corn flakes, relativity, motion pictures, Pyrex glass, and much more were born.

The "Silent Generation," people born between 1928 and 1945, endured the Great Depression, World War II, and harsh racial segregation. They knew of suffering and sacrifice for a shared purpose that subsequent generations have not known. They knew of insecurity and loss. Theirs is a perspective of counting your blessings and not expecting too much. Theirs is a perspective of electrification, the growing ubiquity of telephones, network television, and the advent of commercial aviation with United Airlines and Pan American just getting started.

What would we call the mobilizing of the generations of Baby Boomers (1946-1964), Gen Xers (1965-1980), Millennials (1981-1996) and Gen Zers (1997-2012) into a united bucket brigade of empowered climate activism? The Great Convergence?

Whatever it is called, may it be so. Such a merger of purpose, resolve, and sacrifice would leave an unforgotten legacy. Humanity and its future generations would know in hindsight that there was everything to gain and very little to lose from re-wilding and de-carbonizing at light-speed scale. The Great Convergence, starting with the *Climate Emergency Credit Card*, may seem impossible, but I am certain that it is not.

I know that we, that is you and me, are the impossible that will not fail us.

Hence, my challenge and my reason to write this *Climate Emergency Plan* is to reach out again to the many who might recognize the ember I am trying to fan, see its potential, and help transform it into the climate revolution we need today.

Acknowledgements

Throughout this *Climate Emergency Plan*, I hammered the point that climate activism, as currently configured and operating, has us faltering. We are losing the global warming battle. Although this determination is not conjured up from my own lay judgments, but rather the assessment of experts and activists like Bill McKibben, I fear that one of the take-aways from my effort is that I am disparaging the many who are dedicating their actions, their dollars, and are doing their best over many decades now to respond to this crisis.

I tried to dispel this take-away throughout the body of this Plan, because it is not the case. But I may have failed.

Hence, I want to acknowledge the climate activists, environmental organizations and their leadership, the millions of contributing members to those environmental organizations, the scientists, journalists, podcasters, educators, researchers, politicians, philanthropists, financial institutions, authors, celebrities, global conference organizers and the many others who have been striving to create the necessary impact to make a difference.

In fact, they are making a difference, "the" difference, because the groundwork has been laid, to bring something like the *PARALLEL* Economy and Climate Activist Movement into reality.

All of the ingredients are on the table. Who will recognize them, measure and mix them in the right proportions and in the right way to make the transformative movement hundreds of millions are waiting for?

In anticipation of this "who," I would like to acknowledge this, to be named, amazing group of leaders who are on their way, betwixt and between, in that Star Trek transporter room. Please announce yourselves. There is no time to lose.

My brother Arnie Koss is a true believer in this *Climate Emergency Plan* and has been relentless in his support to improve upon my first effort. I have needed this support. It truly is a lonely pursuit when you think that you are touching on something important, albeit imperfectly, but yet remain invisible and irrelevant to those you are yearning to reach.

My friend David Fried has remained a stalwart champion of this *Climate Emergency Plan*. Why does he get it? I wish I could discover the answer, bottle it, and give it away for free.

I want to thank again Bill McKibben. My recognition, by happenstance, of his name in the April 2019 open letter to the British daily newspaper, The Guardian, started this *Climate Emergency Plan* ball rolling. And my respect for his determined contributions as a Climate activist and educator grabbed me by the scruff of my neck and dragged me to a heightened awakening of the global warming perils descending upon us.

Finally, I want to acknowledge the skepticism and resistance that my sons, Gabe and Aaron, maintained throughout my writing efforts. They pushed me to understand their perspective and to keep trying to make this *Climate Emergency Plan* relevant. I can't say that I succeeded in winning them over, but I do know their candor energized me to anticipate their criticisms and answer the questions I imagined would keep them forever on the sidelines and apart from this hopeful future their father has imagined for them.

Addendum

The Climate Emergency Credit Card

"Two existential crises are developing with terrifying speed, climate breakdown and ecological breakdown; neither is being addressed with the urgency needed to prevent our life support systems from spiraling into collapse."

> April 3, 2019 letter to *The Guardian Newspaper* signed by 23 of the world's leading climate activists including Bill McKibben, Greta Thunberg, and Naomi Klein.

The stage is set.

The threat of climate catastrophe is upon us. Traditional forms of activism are failing. Relatively few belong to environmental organizations. Millions are sitting on the sidelines as disempowered spectators, struggling with inaction, isolated from each other across the globe, and feeling resigned.

There are plenty of "moments" of sporadic activism like *Strike for the Climate* and *Extinction Rebellion*. Climate awareness is growing. Greta Thunberg is becoming a household name. But there is no everyday 24-7 global climate "movement." There is nothing unifying and empowering for the majority sitting on the sidelines to trust, believe in and connect to. And it is exactly this everyday connection that is needed to unleash the human potential that might prevent our life support systems from spiraling into collapse.

We need a movement.

Introducing the Climate Emergency Credit Card

This is a big idea. Big ideas are the only ones that can really tackle the climate crisis.

Consumption is arguably the root of ecological decline. It is counter-intuitive to suggest a credit card as the point of a climate-activism spear. But the end of consumption is not a feasible solution to the climate emergency. The question then is, how do we make the *"buying of things,"* which everyone does, work for re-wilding the planet and de-carbonizing our everyday lives?

The answer is the Climate Emergency Credit Card, the first global card that is dedicated 100% to fighting climate change.

The possibility of having a big part of our everyday mundane life, that is the *"buying of things,"* become a part of the fight for the climate is a powerful prospect. Multiply that possibility by tens of millions of cardholders and you have, ready to harness, a vast amount of untapped human potential (and capital).

Add to that potential the focus of bringing more understanding/consciousness to the impact of the *"buying of things"* by showcasing (via the *climate emergency card.org* website) new information and perspectives that result in better choices for the planet and we've taken an important step forward.

Every time the *Climate Emergency Card* is used, and it is a strikingly beautiful green card, it makes a statement. It stands for a hopeful future. You know every possible dollar is being funneled to credible and well-vetted efforts to meet the climate change crisis. It offers and reinforces everyday meaning and connection to the greater good.

The First Climate Emergency Bank

To create this Credit Card dedicated 100% to fighting climate change, we also need a not-for-profit bank standing behind it, also 100% dedicated. Imagine, *The First Climate Emergency Bank.* This virtual (no bricks and mortar) initiative provides a means to be independent of the for-profit demands of commercial banks that by definition must direct most of their profits to stockholders.

Together and for the first time, the Climate Emergency Bank and Card will create a vehicle for anyone and everyone to become instantaneously connected and unified as an "activist" community fighting for the climate.

Instead of serving its stockholders as most banks must do and placating its cardholders with frequent flyer miles and cash back rewards as most credit cards do, the Climate Emergency Bank and Card exclusively serve ecological restoration and de-carbonizing; serve our planet and every critter on it; and serve our children and theirs into the future.

<u>Not for Profit</u>

This means that after covering administrative expenses, all proceeds from interest, card processing fees, membership fees and investments will be directed to funding critical environmental efforts.

Also importantly, the aim of the *First Climate Emergency Bank* and the CLEM card is not to reinvent the wheel and become another environmental organization, with all the associated overhead, competing for members and scarce funding dollars. Quite the opposite.

The aim is rather to mobilize engagement, catalyze action, inspire community and be an ally and collaborator everywhere possible for climate activism including being a potential funder for projects initiated by established groups like *Green Peace, 350.org, Sierra Club* and *World Wildlife*.

<u>A means to Create the "Urgency Needed"</u> There are many "feel good" credit cards offered by established organizations like the *World Wildlife Fund (WWF), Sierra Club* and *Green Peace.* These Affinity Card Programs, as they are commonly called, are sponsored by the largest for-profits banks. The WWF Card, for example, from Bank of America authorizes the payment of 0.08% of net retail purchases to the organization. WWF receives $800 for every million dollars of purchases. Also received by WWF is $3.00 for each card subscriber and annual card renewal.

These contributory schemes, although well meaning, are constrained by commercial banking realities. They do not represent the "urgency needed" to prevent our life support systems from spiraling into collapse.

Conversely, the Climate Emergency Bank and Credit Card will create a dedicated platform to specifically express that urgency needed. In doing so, it will capture billions of consumer dollars and re-direct them towards the fight for the planet and for future generations.

These dollars will represent a burgeoning climate activist movement, united at first by merely a shared green credit card held in millions of wallets but ultimately united by the experience of shared empowerment as each cardholder begins to experience the impact upon the world that their everyday ordinary lives is a part of.

Economic Accessibility

The ethos of the *Climate Emergency Card* is to be accessible to as many people as possible. The actual program details to do this will be fleshed out in a creative business plan development process. But conceptually and for illustration purposes, it is easy to imagine a card committed to:

- Low annual membership fees at the discretion of the cardholder: $0 — $40 — $80 — $120
- Low interest intro rates for new card holders
- Below market ongoing APR rates
- Online-only bank presence resulting in lower operating costs than traditional brick and mortar banks

Environmental Expertise

A world class team of environmental scientists and activists will be advisors to the *Climate Emergency Card* program. These experts will be responsible for guiding the profits derived from the card's activity to the most impactful projects that champion de-carbonizing and ecological restoration.

Transparency

The bank and credit card operations will be built upon a platform of 100% transparency. Members can engage directly with the organizations they are supporting. CLEM will gather news and provide project updates creating a live feed of climate change news. This will help deepen the sense of participating in a movement and could even develop into something akin to a TV Channel dedicated to climate/environmental news, networking and activism. There is a world of possibilities to explore here.

Founding Leadership Advisory Group

A *Founding Leadership Advisory Group* needs to form to set the momentum to develop a comprehensive *Climate Emergency Credit Card* business plan. This founding group represents wisdom, capacity, resilience, know-how and entrepreneurial spirit.

A hands-on team of banking, regulatory, capital planning, cybersecurity, organizational development, social and digital media, public relations, marketing and entrepreneurial expertise will be formed around the plan which will then serve as the primary selling document to capitalize the start-up.

An *International Scientific Advisory Board* will also be built by leveraging the prominence and engagement of the Founding Leadership Group. This Board will inform key decisions as to what projects to financially support and promote to maximize the impact of the organization.

Summary: A climate emergency is upon us. The life support systems we all depend on and the future for all generations is threatened. The global scale and the related complexities imposing themselves are, if not incomprehensible, then seemingly insurmountable.

Most people are not engaged with the problem. Many are cynical and resigned. Others are concerned but can think of doing little more than recycling and being as environmentally responsible as practical. Some have a more "activist" outlook and support as members organizations like Green Peace and NRDC.

There is plenty of talk and more and more action, but there is no cohesive movement. The urgency needed to meet the crisis is lacking according to the world's leading climate activists. What can be done?

Imagine with us the *First Climate Emergency Bank* and Credit Card. It needs to happen.

About the Author:

Ron Koss is the co-founder of Earth's Best Baby Foods, the first organic baby company in the United States. He was inducted into the Natural Products Industry's "Hall of Legends" in 2018.

Ron is a founding board member (2009) of Global Health Media, the global leader in creating live-action healthcare teaching videos for low resource settings. Partners today include IFRC, Laerdal, Jhpiego, Save the Children, UNICEF, Last Mile Health and many more.

Ron is the co-author of *The Earth's Best Story* published in 2010 by Chelsea Green Publishing and the author of *The Climate Emergency Plan* self-published in 2025.

Ron and family live in Montpelier, Vermont.

www.ingramcontent.com/pod-product-compliance
Lightning Source LLC
Chambersburg PA
CBHW060504280326
41933CB00014B/2851